Emre I Iter
Section D

UVA Law

LEGAL RESEARCH GUIDE: PATTERNS AND PRACTICE

Fourth Edition

By

BONITA K. ROBERTS
Professor of Law
St. Mary's University School of Law

LINDA L. SCHLUETER
Attorney at Law
Member, Texas Bar and District of Columbia Bar (inactive)

2000

LEXIS Publishing™

LEXIS®-NEXIS® • MARTINDALE-HUBBELL®
MATTHEW BENDER® • MICHIE™ • SHEPARD'S®

Library of Congress Cataloging-in-Publication Data

Roberts, Bonita K.
Legal Research Guide: Patterns and Practice / Bonita K. Roberts, Linda L. Schlueter
— 4th ed.
     p.   cm.
ISBN 0-8205-4378-0
Legal research—United States.   I. Schlueter, Linda L. II. Title.
KF240.R63   2000
340'.07'2073—dc21   99-087993
                                                                CIP

Editorial Offices
2 Park Avenue, New York, NY 10016-5675 (212) 448-2000
201 Mission Street, San Francisco, CA 94105-1831 (415) 908-3200
701 East Water Street, Charlottesville, VA 22902-7587 (804) 972-7600
www.lexis.com

(Pub.3085)

TABLE OF CONTENTS

Page

TABLE OF RESEARCH CHECKLISTS

ACKNOWLEDGMENTS

We want to express our thanks to the following individuals who provided the inspiration for this manuscript: Professor David A. Schlueter, for his constant encouragement and support of this project, and Professor Richard Wydick, for his inspiration to say it in simple English.

In addition, our thanks to Lee Unterborn, Reference/Computer Services Librarian and Associate Professor at St. Mary's University School of Law Library, for his assistance on the computer notes. We also wish to thank Caroline Buckley for her secretarial assistance in preparing the manuscript.

PREFACE

The purpose of this book is to provide law students, attorneys, and others doing legal research a simple step-by-step guide to the basic hard copy research processes. The book is not designed as a textbook to give an in-depth explanation of the law and its sources. Rather, this guide should be used when the research processes are unfamiliar to the researcher either through inexperience or insecurity.

To underscore the common patterns in print form legal research, as well as to simplify comprehension of each research process, checklists are located throughout the text and are separately indexed to allow the reader instant access to particular procedures. Specific problems are also used to illustrate each process, enabling the reader to relate better to each step or to follow the process through by using the problem for actual research. Because legal issues are rarely so straightforward as to involve only one research process, some sample problems are used in more than one chapter to demonstrate the interrelationships between research procedures. An appendix provides additional practice problems, accompanied by a brief outline of the research sources.

Although the databases for computer assisted legal research have expanded dramatically since publication of the third edition, unlimited access to material on-line is not yet affordable or available to all researchers. Consequently, many day-to-day research tasks are still more efficiently completed by traditional research methods. The focus of this book, therefore, remains the efficient use of the manual research processes. In this edition, however, there are brief updated "Computer Note" references meant to indicate those options separate from the checklists for manual research. In addition, the Computer Notes have been expanded to include references to the Internet. We have limited the references to Internet cites to what we consider to be reliable and stable addresses that are unlikely to change.

Chapter 1

CASE LAW RESEARCH

§ A OVERVIEW

Everyone who enters law school becomes acquainted with the basic principles of law and legal logic in the substantive courses. The study of substantive law trains the student to recognize the legal issues confronted in practice on a day-to-day basis. An equally important task, however, is to locate the sources of that substantive law. The lawyer, then, needs to analyze carefully each legal problem first to determine what type of law is involved and then to find the law quickly and accurately. The importance of this legal research is underscored by the American Bar Association's Code of Professional Responsibility which requires understanding of both the principles of law and how to find them.[1] Fortunately, legal research is a systematic process that lends itself to a step-by-step approach. The purpose of this guide is to explain and re-enforce these processes through the use of checklists which will help simplify the research process.

THE PATTERN OF LEGAL AUTHORITY			
LEVELS OF AUTHORITY	*Federal*	*State*	*Local*
TYPES OF AUTHORITY	Constitution Statutes Cases Administrative Rules & Regs	Constitution Statutes Cases Administrative Rules & Regs	Municipal Charters Ordinances Administrative Rules & Regs

[1] Types of Authority

The American legal system is comprised of law from several levels of government and various types of authority. Legal authority is divided into two major categories: they are *primary* and *secondary* authority. These types of authority affect the research process because of their relative importance.

[a] Primary Authority

Primary authority is the law itself, and therefore, the most desirable source of legal research. Primary authority consists of written constitutions, statutes, and court decisions. These authorities are in turn designated as either *mandatory* or *persuasive*.

---

[1] Canon 6 of the Code of Professional Responsibility states that lawyers are to know "these plain and elementary principles of law which are commonly known by well-informed attorneys, and to discover the additional rules which, although not commonly known, may readily be found by standard research techniques."

1

Primary mandatory authority consists of the constitution, statutes, and decisions of the highest level of courts from a jurisdiction. For example, all trial and intermediate appellate courts in California must follow the California constitution, statutes, and Supreme Court of California decisions. *Primary persuasive authority* consists of appellate court decisions from other jurisdictions. However, the constitutions or statutes from other jurisdictions are neither mandatory nor persuasive. Because primary authority is the most important source, the researcher should always try to locate such authority to support the client's position.

[b]   Secondary Authority

Secondary authority is all other written expressions of the law. As a rule, secondary authority explains or expounds upon primary authority. It is generally used if there is no primary authority to support or explain the legal issue. Examples of secondary authority include treatises, law review or bar journal articles, and legal encyclopedias.

TYPES OF AUTHORITY	
PRIMARY:	State and Federal Constitution Statutes Cases — either mandatory or persuasive
SECONDARY:	State and Federal All other written expressions of the law

The purpose of this chapter is to analyze *primary authority* in the form of cases, that is, judicial decisions, and to discuss the methods of finding that case law. The following chapters will discuss the other forms of primary and secondary authority.

[2]   The Foundation

The Anglo-American judicial system is founded on the concept of the "common law" and the doctrine of *stare decisis.* The term "common law" refers to the judicial decisions by English courts which were the basis of law for the states and countries originally settled and controlled by England. Thus, the term is distinguished from that body of law from other judicial systems such as Roman law, civil law, and canon law. Because American judicial decisions came from English common law, they are also referred to as the common law. The term, however, does not include statutes that are passed by the various federal and state legislatures.

From this concept of the common law, the doctrine of *stare decisis* emerged. Simply stated, the court will review the facts of "our case" to determine if they are the same or substantially similar to those in previous cases. These earlier cases are referred to as precedent. If the facts are similar, then the same law will be applied. If there are some differences or distinctions in the legally significant facts, then the court will not adhere to the principle of law announced in the precedent. Instead it will apply another rule or create a new rule, which in turn may become precedent for later cases. In some cases, even where the legally significant facts are identical, the court for policy reasons may not follow the precedent. This has the positive effect of adding flexibility to our law when the needs of society change.

The doctrine of *stare decisis* is fundamental to the American judicial system because of three inherent advantages. First, *stare decisis* promotes a sense of stability to our law. This is essential if there is to be public confidence in the judicial system. Second, *stare decisis* provides some predictability of the outcome of the case. It is important for lawyers to be able to advise their clients with confidence, and they can do so with a measure of certainty because of this doctrine. Third, *stare decisis* ensures fairness by the court. This means that individuals will be treated the same way given a certain set of facts. This doctrine is important to the legal researcher because it highlights the emphasis on *case law* to the American legal system. Therefore, every researcher's goal is to find a case "on point." This is the ultimate achievement in legal research!

[3] The Court System

The courts on both the state and federal levels are organized in a similar structure, although the names of the courts may be different in each state. *Trial courts* hear testimony from witnesses or receive written documents as evidence. These courts decide matters of law and fact. As a general rule, trial court decisions are not reported. The exception to this rule is federal district court decisions; however, only 10-15% of these cases are reported.

If the trial court has committed prejudicial error, the case may be appealed to an *intermediate court of appeals.* These courts hear only issues of law and are bound by the facts that were introduced in the trial court. However, only 30-35% of the cases at the federal level are reported because all federal circuits have adopted rules restricting the number of published cases due to the heavy case load.

Some cases may be appealed to the *court of last resort* if there has been prejudicial error by the intermediate court of appeals. It should be emphasized that not all errors are grounds for appeal. The courts are not called upon to be perfect; they only need to be fair. In addition, the court of last resort is limited to questions of law that are presented in written briefs and in some instances oral arguments. All decisions from the court of last resort are reported, although in some instances, decisions involving disciplinary matters may be omitted.

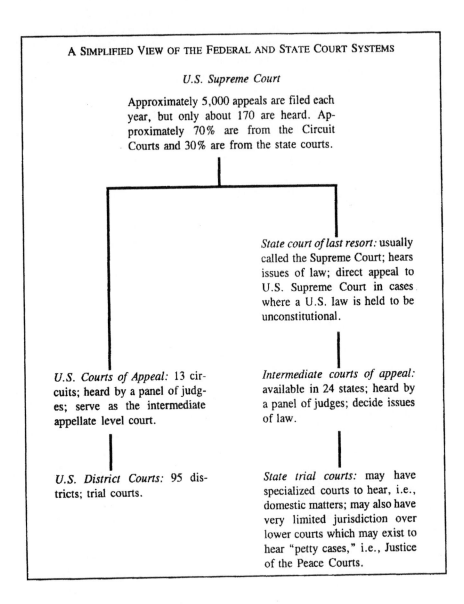

A Simplified View of the Federal and State Court Systems

U.S. Supreme Court

Approximately 5,000 appeals are filed each year, but only about 170 are heard. Approximately 70% are from the Circuit Courts and 30% are from the state courts.

State court of last resort: usually called the Supreme Court; hears issues of law; direct appeal to U.S. Supreme Court in cases where a U.S. law is held to be unconstitutional.

U.S. Courts of Appeal: 13 circuits; heard by a panel of judges; serve as the intermediate appellate level court.

Intermediate courts of appeal: available in 24 states; heard by a panel of judges; decide issues of law.

U.S. District Courts: 95 districts; trial courts.

State trial courts: may have specialized courts to hear, i.e., domestic matters; may also have very limited jurisdiction over lower courts which may exist to hear "petty cases," i.e., Justice of the Peace Courts.

§ B   CASE LAW ORGANIZATION

Before examining the various methods of finding a particular case, it is important to review briefly the ways in which the cases are *reported, i.e.,* published.

[1]   Official and Unofficial Reports

The decisions of the courts that are published are reported in *official* and/or *unofficial* reports. An official report is one that has been designated as such by the federal or state legislature. However, the terms "official" and "unofficial" do not indicate the quality or accuracy of a report. Both forms of publication include cases that have been designated by the court for publication and prepared by the clerk's office. At the present time, 31 states have official reports. If there is an official report of the case, then it *must* be cited in that jurisdiction and it must precede any unofficial cite. For example, a case decided by the Iowa Supreme Court would be cited as follows:

Claude v. Weaver Constr. Co., 261 Iowa 1225, 158 N.W.2d 139 (1968).

In addition, neither the term nor the order of citation reflect the importance or popularity of the reporter. The unofficial reports are by far more popular because they are published more quickly than the official reports and contain many research aids. In contrast, the official reports are very slow in being published and generally do not contain research aids.

[2] The Organization of Reported Cases

Court decisions may be published in three ways: by jurisdiction, by geographical location, or by subject matter.

[a] Jurisdiction

Using this type of organization, cases from a specific court or several courts within a system will be published together. For example, the United States Supreme Court decisions are published in the *United States Reports*. One would not find, for example, the decision of a California court in that publication. The *United States Reports* are the "official" version, but a collection of Supreme Court decisions may also be found in the *Supreme Court Reporter,* an "unofficial" report published by West Group.

[b] Geography

Cases are also reported according to geographic areas. Several states in a regional area can be combined in a single reporter. For example, cases from Texas, Arkansas, Kentucky, Missouri, and Tennessee make up the *Southwestern Reporter*, another publication from West Group.

[c] Subject Matter

Court decisions may also be reported according to subject matter. For example, Tax Court decisions (generally called "memos") and Bankruptcy Court opinions are reported in various looseleaf services for those particular subjects.

[3] The Stages of Publication

To facilitate access to reported decisions, court reports are published in three stages.

[a] Slip Opinions

The quickest form of publication is the "slip opinion" which is issued on the same day as the court announces its opinion. The slip opinion, which is usually in typewritten form, simply reports the decision of a particular case and does not include the syllabus (summary of the case), index, or other research aids that are generally found in later editions. The United States Supreme Court is an example of a court that issues slip opinions. Slip opinions can be obtained from the clerk of the court or sometimes on a subscription basis.

[b] Advance Sheets

"Advance sheets" are the next quickest form of publication. These are paper bound pamphlets which contain a number of cases from a particular jurisdiction and are generally issued on a monthly basis. Several advance sheets in turn comprise one bound volume of a reporter. Advance sheets contain the same research aids, format, and pagination as the bound volume.

[c] Bound Volumes

After some delay, sometimes months or even years, the bound volumes are available. The typical features of a bound volume include: a table of cases, in which the cases are listed both in alphabetical order and according to state in the regional reporters; a table of the statutes that are construed by the cases; the opinions of the court; research aids; a subject index; an index of words and phrases that are defined in the cases; and court rules that are interpreted in the volume.

STAGES OF REPORTING CASES

Slip Opinions

↓

Advance Sheets

↓

Bound Volumes

---

[4] Subject Access

Because cases are published in chronological order in the bound volumes, researchers did not have *subject access* to the law. To remedy this problem, in 1897, John West, founder of West Group, devised a method for subject classification of legal and factual issues. He began by dividing the law into seven major *categories:* persons, property, contracts, torts, crimes, remedies, and government. These seven major categories were then subdivided into more than 400 legal *topics.* These topics were then divided into even more specific sections which were called *key numbers.* This subject arrangement of the law is collected in volumes called *digests.*

The *American Digest System* purports to list every reported state and federal case. It arranges cases according to topics and key numbers and states the principle of law in a short paragraph which is called an *abstract* of the case. Although West periodically adds new topics and key numbers as they are needed, it has maintained the original categories created by John West.

There are several types of digests. To find cases at both the state and federal levels, the *American Digest* should be consulted. Its volumes are divided according to years as follows:

Century Digest	1658 to 1896
First Decennial	1897 to 1906
Second Decennial	1907 to 1916
Third Decennial	1917 to 1926
Fourth Decennial	1927 to 1936
Fifth Decennial	1937 to 1946
Sixth Decennial	1947 to 1956
Seventh Decennial	1957 to 1966
Eighth Decennial	1966 to 1976
Ninth Decennial	1976 to 1986
Tenth Decennial	1986 to 1996

Due to the large volume of cases, the Ninth Decennial was divided into two parts: Part I contains cases from 1976 to 1981 and Part II contains cases from 1981 to 1986. In addition, West introduced new topics and expanded old ones in the Ninth Decennial. Just as the Ninth Decennial was divided into two parts, the Tenth Decennial is also divided: Part I contains cases from 1986 to 1991 and Part II has cases from 1991 to 1996. The disadvantage to the General Digest is that each topic has not been compiled into one volume. Therefore, the researcher must consult numerous volumes which is a very time consuming process.

The *General Digest* is the name for the current decennial before the ten-year period has occurred. For example, what will be the Eleventh Decennial is the current General Digest. It began in 1996 and will go for the next ten-year period.

In addition to the *American Digest System*, West publishes a *state digest* for every state except Delaware, Nevada, and Utah. In those states, the researcher must consult the corresponding regional digest. A state digest contains all state and federal cases reported within that state. In addition, there are "Library References" to *Corpus Juris Secundum (C.J.S.)*, West's legal encyclopedia, as well as "Research Notes" to a few other general publications.

Regional digests are also published for the regional reporters, with three exceptions. The Southwestern and Northeastern regions currently do not have a digest and West ceased publishing the *Southern Digest* in 1988. Access to the cases from these regions can be gained through the respective state digests.

Finally, there are digests for a single court or system of courts. The primary examples of these types of digests are the ones that publish federal cases. There is a series of digests for federal materials that include the *Federal Digest* (contains cases prior to 1939), the *Modern Federal Practice Digest* (1939 to 1961), *Federal Practice Digest 2d* (1962 to 1975), *Federal Practice Digest 3d* (November 1975 to 1989), and *Federal Practice Digest 4th* (1989 to present).

There are several advantages to the digest system. First, the researcher is able to locate all cases on a particular point of law from the earliest time to the present. Second, research can be confined to a limited period of time, *i.e.*, a five- to ten-year period. Third, the search can be as broad as the entire United States or as narrow as a particular state. Fourth, digests list cases regardless of whether they cite each other or not.

However, there are some inherent disadvantages to the digest system. The researcher must keep in mind that these are only abstracts of the cases and not the opinions of the courts or even the holdings of the courts in all abstracts. Furthermore, the abstracts do not indicate whether the case has been overruled or is affected by a statute. Therefore, the *general caveats* in legal research apply to the digests: (a) the case itself *must* be read; (b) only the opinion should be quoted; and, (c) all relevant cases *must* be "Shepardized." The digests are probably the most common means of finding a case, and they can be a valuable research tool when viewed with the proper perspective.

§ C   Case Law Location Methods

The purpose of this section is to demonstrate that legal research is an integrated process whereby numerous resources by various publishers can be used to find the information quickly. Because our legal system is based on the doctrine of *stare decisis,* it is important that the lawyer find a case that is factually similar. There are several methods by which a case can be located depending upon the information the researcher already has. The simplest methods will be described first.

LOOKING FOR A CASE?

Do you have the case name? If so, use one of the following methods:

__ 1. Digest Table of Cases: Listed by the plaintiff's name.

__ 2. *SHEPARD'S Acts and Cases by Popular Names:* Lists cases by their popular name.

__ 3. Digest's Defendant-Plaintiff Table: Listed by the defendant's name.

If you do not have the name of a case, use one of the following methods:

__ 4. Words and Phrases: Lists the definitions of words that have been defined by the court.

__ 5. Digest's Descriptive Word Index: Lists information according to subject matter.

__ 6. Digest's Topic Method: Lists information according to West's topics and key numbers.

__ 7. *American Law Reports (A.L.R.):* Analyzes cases on a narrow issue or topic.

---

[1]   Table of Cases Method

Assume that the researcher only has the name of a case and wants to find a copy of the decision. The simplest technique for finding a case is to go to the *Table of Cases* in a digest which lists all cases in alphabetical order by plaintiff's name. Here is an illustration:

EXAMPLE: Assume that you want to find a Maryland case entitled *Sowell v. State.* Employ the following steps:

     1. *Bound Volume:* Go to the appropriate state or regional digest Table of Cases. In this example, Maryland is in the *Atlantic Digest.* If the digest has more than one series, as does the *Atlantic Digest,* be sure to check the Table of Cases for the most *recent* series because it contains the cases for all series. Check by alphabetical designation of the first name listed. In this example you would look under "S" for Sowell.

     2. *Pocket Part:* If the case is NOT in the bound volume, check the pocket part located in the back of the bound volume. Some digests, like *Atlantic Second Series,* have a Cumulative Pamphlet which supplements the main Table of Cases volumes instead of a pocket part so be sure to check it. *Sowell v. State* can be found in the 1999 cumulative pamphlet.

        When you locate the case name you will also see the jurisdiction followed by the citation to the volume and page number where the case is reported. *Sowell v. State* can be found in volume 712 of the *Atlantic Reporter, Second Series,* on page 96. In addition, the official reporter cite is given, which in this example is volume 122 of *Maryland Appellate Reports* on page 222. Following the citation is a list of topics and key numbers under which the case is classified in the descriptive word index. The Descriptive Word Method will be explained later.

3. *Reporter:* Look up the case in volume 712 of the *Atlantic Reporter, Second Series,* on page 96.

Computer Note

Both **LEXIS®-NEXIS®** and **WESTLAW®** provide databases for federal and state cases. The federal cases include the reported trial, appellate, and United States Supreme Court cases. At the state level, reported appellate cases are on-line. Access to these cases can be gained through several methods. Relevant to this section is a name search in which either the plaintiff's or defendant's name or both may be used. There is also **Internet** access to cases, although there may be limitations depending on the database or court. At the federal level, United States Supreme Court cases from 1893 to present can be found through <http://www.findlaw.com/casecode/supreme.html>. Cases for the thirteen federal Courts of Appeal can be found through <http://www.uscourts.gov/link.html>. At the present time, United States District Court opinions are not available on the web. State court decisions are also available. For example, Texas Supreme Court cases could be accessed through <http://www.supreme.courts.state.tx.us/scopn.html>. Texas Courts of Appeal are available through <http://www.info.courts.state.tx.us/appindex/appindex.exe>.

---

[2] *SHEPARD'S Acts and Cases by Popular Names*

Another set of books that lists cases by name in alphabetical order is *SHEPARD'S Acts and Cases by Popular Names.* This set is different from the Table of Cases in a digest because it does not include all cases. It contains only those cases, state and federal, that have a popular name. A popular name is descriptive of the case but does not usually include the parties' names.

EXAMPLE: Locate the "Black Watch Case." Employ the following steps:

1. *Bound Volume:* Find the bound volume to *SHEPARD'S Acts and Cases by Popular Names* and look in the last volume of the 1992 bound volumes under "Federal and State Cases" cited by popular name for the "Black Watch Case." Check under "B" for "Black Watch Case." You will find the abbreviation for the reporter where the case is located. In this example, it is volume 376 of the *Federal Supplement* beginning on page 1154.

2. *Supplementary Pamphlet:* If the case is not in the bound volume, check the supplementary pamphlet.

3. *Reporter:* Look up the case in volume 376 of the *Federal Supplement* at page 1154.

[3] Defendant-Plaintiff Table

The third means of locating a case by title involves the defendant-plaintiff table. Each federal and state digest provides a list of cases in alphabetical order by defendant's name. Note, however, that regional digests and the *American Digest* (until the Ninth Decennial Digest) *do not* contain a defendant-plaintiff table. When given a case name to research, it is always a good idea to check the defendant-plaintiff table if the case cannot be found in the Table of Cases to eliminate the possibility that the parties' names have been inadvertently reversed.

EXAMPLE: The researcher wants to find a recent Texas case but knows only that the defendant's name is Knuckley. Employ the following steps:

1. *Bound Volume:* Go to the *Texas Digest, Second Series*, Defendant-Plaintiff Table. Use the *Second Series* volumes because you already know that the case is recent and the *Second Series* covers decisions reported since 1935. Look under "K" for Knuckley.

2. *Pocket Part:* Check the pocket part in the back of the bound volume if the case cannot be found in the bound volume. Once the case name is located, a citation to the reporter will be given.

3. *Reporter:* Since you have located the *Knuckley* case in the bound volume of the Defendant-Plaintiff Table, go to volume 637 of the *Southwestern Reporter, Second Series*, page 920, where the case begins.

Computer Note

The researcher can also find the defendant's name on **LEXIS-NEXIS** or **WESTLAW** using the same name search that was used to find the plaintiff's name. If the defendant's name appears in the database, the case will be retrieved. As described in the previous Computer Note, cases can be found on the **Internet** for some courts.

---

[4] *Words and Phrases* Volumes

Whenever the researcher has a definitional problem, the first source to check are the volumes entitled *Words and Phrases*. These volumes appear in two forms. The first and most convenient form is the "permanent edition" of *Words and Phrases* which currently has forty-six volumes in the series. These books help the researcher to locate cases, both state and federal, that have defined a word or phrase. The definitions are arranged in alphabetical order and use abstracts to state the court's definition of a word. In addition, if a word has several related terms, an index to these subordinate matters is listed and the abstracts are arranged according to the index format. For example, if the word to be defined is "jewelry," the index also lists such things as "buckles," "gems," and "pearls." This material is updated through annual cumulative pocket parts in the back of each volume.

The second type of *Words and Phrases* volume is the "digest edition." There are volumes entitled "Words and Phrases" at the end of each series of the state, federal, and specialized digests. These volumes contain the words that have been defined by the courts in that particular state. The disadvantage to the digest editions is that the words only have citations to the cases in which they were defined, and not abstracts of definitions themselves. This information is updated through the annual cumulative pocket part at the back of each volume; the most recent information can be found in the Table of Words and Phrases in the bound volumes and advance sheets of the *National Reporter* system since the last printing of the annual pocket part.

The following problem illustrates the use of *Words and Phrases.*

EXAMPLE: Joe Victim owns a home in Baton Rouge, Louisiana. On May 1, his house was burgled of some tools, electrical appliances, money, and jewelry. The homeowner's insurance policy which was issued by Allspice Insurance Company contained a clause which limited liability for jewelry to $500.00. The insurance company refused to reimburse Joe for his expensive cuff links because they were considered "jewelry" and were valued at $850.00. Joe contends that they are not jewelry but "functional items" which are not subject to the limitation clause. According to Louisiana case law, are cuff links considered "jewelry"? Use the following research steps:

1. The researcher should use the *Words and Phrases* volumes in either the *Louisiana Digest* or the *Words and Phrases* permanent edition.

2. *Bound Volume:* Locate the bound volume in the permanent edition for "jewelry." For this example, however, there are no cases on point in the bound volume.

3. *Pocket Part:* However, there is a case on point in the pocket part under the term "jewelry" and subpart "in general." That case is *Halford v. Republic Underwriters Ins. Co.,* 348 So. 2d 87 (La. App. 4th Cir. 1977), which states that cuff links are jewelry. This problem highlights an important research point: the researcher must always follow the proper updating procedures, such as checking the pocket parts so that pertinent cases are not overlooked.

4. *Reporter:* Further updating should be done through the bound volumes and advance sheets of the *Southern Reporter* that have been printed since the last pocket part to *Words and Phrases* was published.

5. *Shepardize:* Any relevant case, *Halford* in this example, should be Shepardized to ensure that it has not been overruled or modified.

Before a case can be cited as authority, the researcher must verify that it is still "good law," *i.e.*, that the case has not been reversed, overruled, modified, or excessively criticized. This final check is made by Shepardizing the case in the appropriate volumes of *SHEPARD'S®*. This final step in legal research is a *must.* On occasion, there are cases in the reporters where the court will reprimand counsel for not knowing that a case he has cited as authority has been overruled. This embarrassment can easily be avoided if the researcher remembers that the last step in legal research is to Shepardize all cases that are going to be cited as authority.

There are *SHEPARD'S* volumes that correspond to each of the state and regional reporters. It is helpful to check both *SHEPARD'S* volumes, because each volume contains different information. For example, the state *SHEPARD'S* contain references to *American Law Reports* (*A.L.R.*) annotations, law reviews, and Attorney General Opinions. Regional *SHEPARD'S* contain cites to *A.L.R.* annotations and citations to cases in other jurisdictions that have cited this case. There may also be differences in the publication date. The regional *SHEPARD'S* may be more current because of the differences in publishing the official and unofficial reports as discussed earlier.

To Shepardize a case, the researcher should follow these steps:

(1) Find the appropriate set of *SHEPARD'S*.

(2) Several books will be on the shelf so it is critically important to find the volume(s) that correspond to the reporter. Frequently, the first-year law student fails to check if the volume of *SHEPARD'S* corresponds to the first or second series of the reporter. If the researcher is in the wrong volume of *SHEPARD'S,* then the case has not been Shepardized.

(3) The listings are in numerical order by volume and then page number. Find the case by the appropriate numerical cite.

(4) Review the history of the case as well as the treatment of other cases. *SHEPARD'S* indicates this by a small letter prior to the citation to the reporter. In the front of each *SHEPARD'S* volume, there is a list of abbreviations. For example, "s" means it is the same case at a different level of proceeding, *i.e.*, trial level or appellate level; "r" means reversed; "a" means affirmed; and "d" means distinguished.

(5) The small raised letters after the reporter abbreviation correspond to the headnote number in the case. The researcher can save time by looking specifically to find the relevant headnote.

(6) Be sure to check all bound volumes and supplements to *SHEPARD'S* where the case may appear. Each pamphlet *must* be checked or else the researcher has not Shepardized.

Use *Halford v. Republic Underwriters Ins. Co.*, 348 So. 2d 87 (La. App. 4th Cir. 1977) as an example. At the present time, there are fifteen bound volumes of *SHEPARD'S* for the *Southern Reporter, First* and *Second Series.* Volume 2, part 6 would contain volume 348 So. 2d in it. Using that volume, turn to the page where 348 So. 2d 87 would appear. The first entry has an "s" before the cite 350 So. 2d 1214, which means that this is the decision of a higher level court. If you check this cite, you will discover that on October 26, 1977, the Supreme Court of Louisiana denied a writ of review. In addition, there is a two-part 1994-1999 bound supplement which potentially has the *Halford* case in part 1. Check the pamphlets to determine if the court of appeals decision has been cited in more recent court decisions.

Computer Note

Effective July 1, 1999, Shepardizing is only available through **LEXIS-NEXIS**. Since acquiring *SHEPARD'S*, **LEXIS-NEXIS** has made some improvements in the format and capabilities of *SHEPARD'S* which make it easier and more productive for the researcher to use. **WESTLAW** has created its on-line citation service which is called KEYCITE®. Through a system of flags and stars, it warns the researcher of negative history and the depth of the court's treatment. Because KEYCITE is new, only time will tell whether it is as good a tool as *SHEPARD'S*.

---

[5] Descriptive Word Method

There are three easy ways to find the appropriate topic and key number. The first is the *Table of Cases Method* (discussed above). Using this method, the researcher locates the appropriate headnote from a known relevant case. The headnote states the topic and key number and this information can then be used in the digest system. The *Descriptive Word Method* and the *Topic Method* will be discussed below.

FINDING A TOPIC AND KEY NUMBER

1. Table of Cases Method
2. Descriptive Word Method
3. Topic Method

The *Descriptive Word Method* is the most common starting point if the researcher simply has a fact situation with no leads from a relevant case or statute. The first step in finding a case is to analyze accurately and thoroughly your fact situation. Your analysis should center around five elements which are common to every case. These elements are:

1. *Parties:* These are persons of a particular class, occupation, or relationship. Examples of parties might be tenants, doctors, children, heirs, or any person who is necessary for the lawsuit to be resolved.

2. *Places and Things:* These are objects which are involved in the dispute or have caused the problem to exist, or places where the problem arose. These may include automobiles, sidewalks, public buildings, theatres, or amusement parks.

3. *Basis of the Action or Issue:* This category considers the wrong suffered by reason of another's neglect of duty, some affirmative wrong that was committed, some legal obligation that was ignored, or the violation of a statutory or constitutional provision. Examples include negligence, conversion of property, a violation of the child labor laws, or an illegal search and seizure.

4. *Defenses:* This category reviews the reasons in law or fact why the plaintiff should not recover. Act of God, assumption of the risk, or infancy are some examples of defenses.

5. *Relief Sought:* This category analyzes the legal remedy that is sought by the plaintiff. For example, the plaintiff may seek punitive damages, annulment, or an injunction.

Each of these categories should be analyzed in detail. Try to think of as many different words as you can for each category. In selecting key words and phrases, think of synonyms, antonyms, or closely related words. If you are having difficulty thinking of different words, use a dictionary or thesaurus. It should also be noted that, depending on the problem, some categories will be more helpful than others. Examine a problem that illustrates this point:

EXAMPLE: Assume the jurisdiction is Colorado. Defendant was convicted of and sentenced for burglary. He was caught in the act of prying the lid off the coin box of an outside telephone booth. The booth was located about twenty-five feet from a gas station. The defendant has argued that he should not have been convicted of burglary because a telephone booth is not a "building" within the meaning of the state statute on burglary. Under Colorado case law, is an outside telephone booth considered a "building"? Find all case law on point.

Using the recommended case analysis, the key words and phrases should be used to describe the parties, places and things, basis of the action or issue, defenses, and the relief sought. Some of the words and phrases that might be used are as follows:

1. *Parties:* burglar, criminal, state of Colorado

2. *Places and Things:* coin box, telephone booth, gasoline station

3. *Basis of the Action or Issue:* meaning of building, burglary, criminal act or law

4. *Defenses:* telephone booth is not a building

5. *Relief Sought:* acquittal, reversal of the conviction

As noted above, not all of the words in our analysis will be helpful nor will every category of words or phrases be helpful in a particular problem. Therefore, the researcher should begin with the *most specific* key words. If these words are too specific, then more general words can be used. For example, the categories of parties, defenses, and relief sought are not helpful in this problem. The more specific terms that form the places and things and basis of the action categories are significant.

The researcher should go to the *Pacific Digest Descriptive Word Index.* The word "telephone booth" has a subheading of burglary and refers the researcher to the topic "burglary" and the key number 4. Under the word "burglary," there is a listing for "telephone booth." This notation refers the researcher to the same *topic and key number.*

Other words and phrases such as "criminal act or law" and "acquittal" are too general to be helpful. The word "building" is more specific but still will not be listed in the digest as a separate item. Also, the word "coin box" is very specific but the subheading leads the researcher to "larceny by taking from paid telephones," the topic "Criminal Law," and key numbers 419(10) and 448(7). These are not helpful in this problem because they both deal with evidence matters, *i.e.,* evidence regarding a defendant taking money from a coin box in a telephone booth. This information is not relevant to the narrow question presented in this problem. When you find a certain topic and key number through several relevant words and phrases, such as "Burglary 4," then you can be certain that you have found the appropriate one.

Once the topic and key number have been found, the researcher should *go to the digest.* The researcher should notice that most digests are now in the second series. Since a particular date does not limit the problem, start with the most recent series. Unlike some digests, the *Pacific Digest* does not designate a first, second, or third series but instead indicates the beginning volumes of the *Pacific Reporter.* The following digests exist for the *Pacific Reporter:*

Starting 1 P.	1830 to 1931
Starting 1 P.2d	1931 to 1940
Starting 101 P.2d	1940 to 1962
Starting 367 P.2d	1962 to 1978
Starting 585 P.2d	1978 to present

A researcher looking in the present *Pacific Digest* under "Burglary 4" would find no cases on point. Therefore, the researcher would have to go to the prior edition which starts with 367 P.2d. In that edition under "Burglary 4," the researcher would find the case of *Macias v. People,* 161 Colo. 233, 421 P.2d 116 (1966), where the court held that a telephone booth could not be the subject of a burglary, and, therefore, the defendant was not guilty of burglary.

Once the *bound volume* has been reviewed, it is important for the researcher to update the information. Law books are constantly being updated. Therefore, the researcher must ask: "How is this volume supplemented or updated?" The digests are updated by *pocket parts.* In this problem, the pocket part for the volume should be checked, but there are no further cases on point. In addition, there may be a semi-annual supplementary pamphlet for newer editions. These also should be checked. For example, there is a May and September supplementary pamphlet for the *Pacific Digest* beginning with 585 P.2d.

The research is not complete without reviewing earlier digests. Therefore, looking in the volumes for 1940 to 1962 under "Burglary 4," the researcher would find another Colorado case, *Sanchez v. People,* 142 Colo. 58, 349 P.2d 561 (1960). This case also supports the proposition that the defendant is not guilty of burglary. Reviewing the pocket part for this volume produces no new cases. Likewise, reviewing the other two digests and their pocket parts do not reveal any other supporting cases in Colorado. To complete the research process, the researcher must Shepardize relevant cases in the appropriate *SHEPARD'S*. By way of review, the following summarizes the research steps that are involved in this problem:

    (a) Analyze the fact situation according to the parties, places and things, basis of the action, defenses, and relief sought in order to isolate key words or phrases.

    (b) Use these key words in the Descriptive Word Index.

    (c) The pocket part for the index must be checked for new entries.

    (d) The specific volume of the digest must be checked for cases that are on point.

    (e) In addition, the problem indicates that all case law must be found. Therefore, it is necessary to examine all relevant digests.

    (f) The pocket part of each digest should also be checked for the latest cases.

    (g) For thorough research, the date of the pocket part should be noted so that the topic and key number can be run in the relevant General Digest volume and the advance sheets of the regional reporter.

    (h) Read the relevant cases.

(i)   Relevant cases must be Shepardized in the proper volume of *SHEPARD'S* to ensure that they have not been overruled or modified.

In summary, this exercise demonstrates several important research points. First, it is important to learn how to analyze your facts so that you can isolate key words and phrases which will lead you to similar cases. Under the doctrine of *stare decisis,* this becomes a critical factor. Second, when a relevant topic and key number are located, they may be used in different digests. In this example, we went from a newer digest to an older one. However, the same principle is possible if we begin in a state digest and want to expand our research to a regional or national digest. Finally, it is imperative that the researcher update the information and Shepardize relevant cases.

Computer Note

Through a combination of key words and phrases, the researcher is able to do a subject-matter search for cases on **LEXIS-NEXIS** and **WESTLAW**. In addition to key words and phrases, the researcher can now use "freestyle" on **LEXIS-NEXIS** and "natural language" on **WESTLAW** which simplifies the research query. The search may be limited to one jurisdiction, such as Colorado in our previous example, or expanded to a regional or national search. **WESTLAW** also provides access to West's digest system so that the researcher can do a search by topic and key number.

---

[6]   Topic Method

Another method of finding a case in a digest is the *Topic Method.* As soon as the researcher becomes familiar with the topics that are used by West, it is possible to search for the most specific topic. Once that is found, the researcher can read the *"scope note"* which is provided by West to double check the analysis. The scope note indicates what material is covered within the topic. West also provides a *topic analysis* which is like a table of contents of the topic and key number subjects. From this analysis, the researcher can select the most appropriate key number.

We may use the same burglary problem to demonstrate that the same cases can be found using the Topic Method. By searching the 435 topics, the researcher would discover that the topic of Burglary was the most relevant topic. Turning to that section, the researcher would then review the *scope note* which states in part the "Nature and extent of criminal responsibility therefor and grounds of defense." It would appear that this is the relevant topic.

Further inquiry of the topic would lead the researcher to the analysis section where the contents of the topic Burglary are outlined. Review of the contents would lead the researcher to Part I which is entitled "Offenses and Responsibility therefor." Still more specific information is given and the key number 4 is described as "character of building."

Review our discussion of the digests and locating relevant cases by a checklist of steps to remember.

DIGEST CHECKLIST

1. Analyze the fact situation according to the parties, places and things, basis of the action, defenses, and relief sought in order to isolate key words or phrases.

2. Locate the relevant topic and key number by:

    a. using the plaintiff's name in the Table of Cases;

    b. using the defendant's name in the Defendant-Plaintiff Table;

    c. using key words and phrases in the Descriptive Word Index; or

    d. analyzing the topics according to the Topic Method.

3. Use the relevant topic and key number through all the relevant state, regional, or federal digests.

4. Update the digest through:

    a. the pocket part;

    b. the supplementary pamphlet, if any;

    c. the appropriate volumes of the General Digest; and

    d. the advance sheets of the regional reporter.

5. Read the relevant cases.

6. Shepardize the relevant cases.

---

[7] *American Law Reports (A.L.R.)*

[a] **Overview of *A.L.R.***

The same cases found by the digest method can be found through the *American Law Reports*. The *American Law Reports* (*A.L.R.*) are a series of annotated reports that are published by West Group. This selective reporter of appellate court decisions is one of the major research tools for finding case law. The goal of the *A.L.R.* is to analyze only selected cases. Thus, in 1919, *A.L.R.* was created to provide lawyers with a continuing series of up-to-date annotations that would collect, organize, and evaluate all of the case law relevant to a specific and narrow point of law or fact situation.

A.L.R. is published in five series and a federal series. In addition, the publisher has developed a series of books that is called the *Total Client-Service Library*. This Library consists of an encyclopedia, form books, and other research and trial preparation aids. These books will be discussed in more detail in Chapter 8 concerning secondary authority.

Each series of *A.L.R.* was published during a limited time frame. *A.L.R.* (the first series) was published between 1919 to 1948 in 175 volumes. Most of these articles have been superseded by more recent annotations. Therefore, a researcher using this series must be sure to follow proper updating procedure. *A.L.R.2d* was published from 1948 to 1965 in 100 volumes. Again, the researcher must be sure to update any cases found in this series. *A.L.R.3d* was published in 1965 to 1980 in 100 volumes. For the first four years, *A.L.R.3d* contained both state and federal issues. However, in 1969, a new series was created, *A.L.R. Federal*, and now all federal materials are contained in this series. Beginning in 1980, *A.L.R.4th* was created and it contains only state topics. *A.L.R.4th* was published from 1980 to 1991 and has 90 volumes. A new fifth series was created in 1992.

Over the years, the format of the annotations has evolved, but most of the following research aids will be found in *A.L.R.2d, 3d, 4th,* and *5th*:

(1) A *reported case*. This case precedes the annotation and illustrates the principles that are involved in the annotation. The case includes a summary of the decision, the procedural evolution of the case, headnotes (different from the ones by West), a highlight of the attorneys' briefs, and the court's decision.

(2) At the beginning of the annotation is a box which refers the researcher to the relevant resources in the *Total Client-Service Library*.

(3) The *scheme* of the annotation outlines what is covered and lists the major topics by their section number.

(4) A *word index* helps the researcher quickly find relevant cases. As with the digest, it is helpful to have analyzed your fact situation and have in mind key words and phrases. The index contains both legal and common words such as things, acts, persons, and places.

(5) The *Table of Jurisdictions* provides quick access to cases from a particular state. For example, if the researcher were searching for only Texas cases, the Table of Jurisdictions would quickly show whether there were any Texas cases in the annotation. If there were, it would list the particular section number within the annotation. In *A.L.R. Federal*, this table is called the *Table of Courts and Circuits*. So if the researcher wanted to find only Fifth Circuit cases, the Table would give that information.

(6) The "*Scope*" section of the text discusses the exact issue that is presented in a particular annotation. If a corollary point is "not included," then the researcher is referred to the proper annotation in one of the other series of books. In addition, information about previous or superseded annotations are noted.

(7) The section entitled "*Related Matters*" cites other secondary authorities. These might include law review articles or treatises on the subject.

(8) The *"Summary"* concisely states the law governing the annotated subject and provides relevant background materials.

(9) The *"Practice Pointers"* section provides useful hints to the attorney in proceeding with the case. These insights are given for both parties and may include ideas for alternative theories of recovery or defenses.

(10) Finally, the *text* of the annotation provides an in-depth and impartial analysis of the issue supported by relevant cases. It notes any applicable rules, the weight of the authority, and any trends. It should be emphasized that *A.L.R.* is only a case finder, and therefore, relevant cases must be read before they are cited.

[b] Finding an *A.L.R.* Annotation

Finding an *A.L.R.* annotation is a relatively easy task. There are three methods of locating an annotation, depending upon the information the researcher already has.

LOOKING FOR AN *A.L.R.* ANNOTATION?

Use one of the following methods:

__ 1. *A.L.R. Index:* Analyze the fact situation according to the parties, places and things, basis of the action, defenses, and relief sought in order to isolate key words or phrases.

__ 2. *A.L.R. Digest Method:* Use the same method described in method 1.

__ 3. *Table of Laws and Regulations:* Use only for *A.L.R. Federal* when the title and section of a federal statute or federal rule and regulation is available and you want to locate an annotation on point.

A.L.R. Index Method

The most common approach for locating an annotation is through the *A.L.R. Index* which replaced the *Index to Annotations* and the *Quick Index* for *A.L.R.2d, 3d, 4th,* and *Federal.* Prior to 1986, the researcher had to go to the most recent *Quick Index*, and then if necessary work backwards to the earlier indices until an annotation was found.

In 1986, the *Index to Annotations* eliminated this time-consuming process because it covered *A.L.R.2d, 3d, 4th, Federal,* the *United States Supreme Court Reports,* and the *Lawyers Edition 2d.* In 1993, a revised and expanded six volume *A.L.R. Index* replaced the five-volume *Index to Annotations.* Now the researcher only needs to search one index rather than five separate indices. In addition, the *A.L.R. Index* provides greater depth of coverage, including more main headings and references. However, the *A.L.R. Index* does not cover *A.L.R.*'s first series, so that the *Quick Index* still needs to be checked. In 1999, the *A.L.R. Index* was updated and revised. Furthermore, a single volume *Quick Index* for 2000 provides references to all annotations in *A.L.R.3d, 4th,* and *5th.* For coverage of *A.L.R.2d, Federal,* and *Lawyers Edition 2d,* the researcher still needs to check the *A.L.R. Index.*

EXAMPLE: Locate both an annotation and the two cases you found through the digest method on the issue of whether a telephone booth is a "building" within the meaning of the Colorado burglary statute.

The researcher should use the recommended case analysis and select the key words and phrases to describe the parties, places and things, basis of the action or issue, defenses, and relief sought. Again, the researcher should begin with the most specific key words in the *A.L.R. Index.* "Telephone booth" is the most specific phrase in the problem but produces no listing. Likewise, the heading "telephone" leads to the heading "telecommunications" which is not helpful.

The next step is to try a more general term such as "burglary" or "buildings." For example, under "burglary," the researcher will find an appropriate annotation listing under the more specific words "building" or "house." Both of these listings lead to 78 A.L.R.2d 778 and 68 A.L.R.4th 425. Under the Index entry for "buildings," the researcher finds a listing for burglary which leads to the same two annotations.

Digest Method

There is a separate digest for *A.L.R.* and *A.L.R.2d,* as well as a combined digest for *A.L.R.3d, 4th, 5th,* and *Federal.* These digests arrange references to annotations by broad topics with cites to annotations and brief synopses to cases within the annotations.

Using the example above, the annotations can be found through the digest method. Since the topic method involves broad subject areas, the phrase "telephone booth" again is too narrow for the research example, but the terms "building" and "burglary" should be checked in the *A.L.R. Digest* for *A.L.R.3rd, 4th, 5th,* and *Federal.* Under burglary, the researcher will find an entry under "Generally" which defines what is a building or house and leads to 68 A.L.R.4th 425. However, the term "buildings" in the *A.L.R. Digest* refers to building construction, maintenance, and repair issues rather than burglary issues, although there is a listing for "what is a building." Thus, it is not helpful. There is a pocket part for this digest and it should also be checked. In the *A.L.R.2d Digest,* the word "burglary" will provide reference to the same annotation located by the *A.L.R. Index* research method by looking at § 2 for "Breaking and entry."

Table of Laws and Regulations Method

This method is inapplicable in this instance because it involves researching federal material, whereas the example focuses on a state statute. However, given another scenario, the Table, which is located in the last volume of the *A.L.R. Index,* would show where federal statutes, regulations, court rules, uniform and model acts, restatements of law, and professional codes of ethics are cited in annotations for *A.L.R. 3d, 4th, 5th, Federal*, and *Lawyers Edition 2d*.

[c] Updating an Annotation

1. *Read and Analyze the Annotation:* Once an annotation has been found, read the text and check the research aids such as the Scope of the Annotation, Related Matters, Practical Pointers, and Table of Jurisdictions.

2. *The Table of Jurisdictions:* Colorado cases are listed within two particular portions of the annotation — § 2 under "General principles" and § 3 under "Booths." One of these cases is *Sanchez v. People*, 142 Colo. 58, 349 P.2d 561 (1960) and is noted under both § 2 and § 3. This is the same case that was located earlier in this chapter through the *Pacific Digest*. It should also be noted that *Sanchez v. People* is the lead case for this annotation.

3. *History Table:* Check the History Table in the back of the last volume of the *A.L.R. Index* by volume and page number of the annotation to determine whether is has been supplemented or superseded. The annotation at 78 A.L.R.2d 778 has been superseded by 68 A.L.R.4th 425. This means that the older annotation has been replaced by the newer one. The *Sanchez* case is noted at § 51 for "telephone booth — outdoor."

4. *Pocket Part:* The final step in updating the annotation is to check the Annotation History Table in the pocket part of the *A.L.R. Index*, again by volume and page number.

[d] Updating the Case Law

Updating the case law is another important step in the process to find more recent case law relevant to the annotation. Note that the update process is different for each series in the *A.L.R.* Check the chart at the end of this chapter for the specific details of each series. For this example, use the following steps:

1. *Bound Volume:* Locate the bound volume of the *A.L.R.2d Later Case Service*. This set provides more recent case law for *A.L.R.2d* annotations by volume and page number of the annotation itself. After finding the appropriate volume that covers 78 A.L.R.2d and the listing for page 778, the researcher will find more case law arranged by paragraph numbers in the original annotation. Since paragraph three of the annotation referred to the *Sanchez* case, a check under the same paragraph in the *Later Case Service* reveals *Macias v. People*, 161 Colo. 233, 421 P.2d 116 (1966). This is the other case that was located by updating the *Pacific Digest*.

2. *Pocket Part:* Check the annual pocket part of the *Later Case Service,* using the same method described above.

3. *Reporter:* Once the case law is located, read the decision in the *Pacific Reporter.*

4. *Shepardize:* All relevant cases must be Shepardized in the appropriate *SHEPARD'S* set.

Computer Note

Except for the first series, *A.L.R.* annotations are available through **LEXIS-NEXIS** and **WESTLAW**. There are several ways that a reference to *A.L.R.* can be found by using **LEXIS-NEXIS**. First, through key words and phrases that may appear in the title, a specific annotation may be found. If a full-text search were done, the words may lead to other unrelated issues. Second, if GENFED library, OMNI file, or the STATE library OMNI file is used, **LEXIS-NEXIS** will automatically retrieve annotations meeting the search specifications. However, **LEXIS-NEXIS** usually has an extra charge for seeing the annotation. Finally, if the researcher finds a case and uses the Auto-Cite command, all annotations citing the case are listed. **WESTLAW** has also added ALR as a database and it is updated every two weeks.

Starting with the 5th series, *A.L.R.* added an "Electronic Search Query" in its "Research Sources" at the beginning of the annotation to aid the researcher in finding additional cases. Sample queries are done for **LEXIS-NEXIS** and **WESTLAW**. In 1992, Lawyers Cooperative (now West Group) published an interim pamphlet which provided this information for each annotation in the 4th series.

		A.L.R. SUMMARY	
Series	Dates	Find	Update
First	1919-1948	*Quick Index*; *A.L.R. Digest*; Table of Cases	*Blue Book of Supplemental Decisions* and its Supplement Pamphlet; Annotation History Table
Second	1948-1965	*A.L.R. Index*; *A.L.R. Digest*	Later Case Service and its Pocket Part; Annotation History Table
Third	1965-1980	*A.L.R. Index*; *A.L.R. Digest*	Pocket Part; Annotation History Table
Fourth	1980-1991	*A.L.R. Index*; *A.L.R. Digest*	Pocket Part; Annotation History Table
Fifth	1992-Present	*A.L.R. Index*; *A.L.R. Digest*	Pocket Part; Annotation History Table
Federal	1969-Present	*A.L.R. Index*; Table of Laws & Regulations; *A.L.R. Digest*	Pocket Part; Annotation History Table

A.L.R. CHECKLIST

1. Analyze the fact situation to find key words and phrases.
2. Find a relevant annotation by using:
   a. the *A.L.R. Index*;
   b. the *A.L.R. Digest* Method for all series; or
   c. the Table of Laws, Rules, and Regulations in *A.L.R. Federal.*
3. Read all of the annotation or the relevant sections.
4. Update the annotation by:
   a. the *Blue Book of Supplemental Decisions* for *A.L.R.* (first series) and Annotation History Table;
   b. the *Later Case Service* for *A.L.R.2d* and its pocket part and the Annotation History Table; and
   c. the pocket part and Annotation History Table for *A.L.R.3d, 4th, 5th,* and *Federal.*
5. Read all relevant cases.
6. Shepardize all relevant cases.

Chapter 2

UNITED STATES CONSTITUTIONAL LAW RESEARCH

§ A OVERVIEW OF THE LEGISLATIVE SYSTEM

Legislative materials are the second form of primary authority. As discussed in Chapter 1, the main goal of the researcher is to find primary authority to support the client's position. The constitutions and statutes on both the federal and state level constitute such authority.

Federal legislative material is based on the hierarchy of law. This law consists of three tiers. Article 6 of the United States Constitution declares that the Constitution is the supreme law of the land. Thus, the Constitution becomes the first tier of legislative materials. However, the Constitution also enumerates certain powers to Congress in Article 1, Section 8. Using these enumerated powers, Congress passes statutes. This type of legislation forms the second tier. Congress also has the authority to create administrative agencies to make the day-to-day rules and regulations that implement the statutes. These agencies' rules and regulations become the third tier.

HIERARCHY OF AUTHORITY

Constitution

↓

Statutes

↓

Administrative Rules and Regulations

In addition to the legislative enactments, the Constitution implicitly provides a check and balance system that includes the judicial branch of government. This means that the United States Supreme Court and the other created courts have the power to interpret the constitutional, statutory, and administrative rulings.

All of this law has a tremendous impact on legal research. To do a thorough job of legal research, the researcher must find the law on all three tiers as well as any judicial opinions that interpret each of these laws. Due to the volume of material, the beginner may become overwhelmed and conclude that this must be the most difficult form of legal research. However, once the research process becomes more familiar, the researcher begins to understand that researching legislative materials is a relatively straightforward procedure.

Because the United States Constitution is the supreme law of the land, our discussion will begin at this point.

§ B   CONSTITUTIONAL LAW LOCATION METHODS

The initial question that may perplex the researcher is why a constitutional provision is needed. It is apparent that one would try to find such a provision if the client's problem raised a direct constitutional issue. However, a less obvious reason is that the researcher may need to find the authority for a statute or administrative rule or regulation. Whenever there is a question of legislative or administrative authority, the researcher should consider the possibility that the authority is based on a constitutional provision.

There are many treatises, law review articles, and other secondary sources that provide a wealth of information about the historical background of the Constitution and its provisions. The researcher simply needs to be aware that such resources are readily available through the card catalog of any library. However, the text of this section will focus on the other research tools for finding the appropriate constitutional provision and interpretive case law.

The text of the United States Constitution may be found in the codes for federal statutory materials. For example, it may be found in the official publication, the *United States Code (U.S.C.)*. However, the major emphasis of this chapter will be placed on the two unofficial annotated codes, the *United States Code Annotated (U.S.C.A.)* (published by West Group) and the *United States Code Service (U.S.C.S.)* (published by LEXIS Publishing℠), because they are the publications that the researcher most frequently uses due to the research aids that are available and the annotation of judicial opinions.

All three of these codes are organized in the same manner. The constitutional provisions are listed in order of article and section number or amendment numbers. The statutory volumes are arranged according to subject matter and statutes are placed in fifty subject titles. However, the research procedure for finding a provision is the same for all of the codes. Because there are no references to interpretive cases in the *U.S.C.*, the unofficial annotated codes are more commonly used.

There are several important differences between the two unofficial codes because of the different philosophies between West and LEXIS Publishing. West purports to provide comprehensive coverage of all federal and state cases. Also, West will refer the researcher to its publications such as the digests, encyclopedias, practice books, and form books. In contrast, LEXIS Publishing provides fewer cases but longer abstracts and will refer the researcher to the Total Client Service Library which contains mostly secondary authority.

LOOKING FOR A U.S. CONSTITUTIONAL PROVISION?

Does the subject matter raise a constitutional issue; is there a statute that implements the Constitution; or is the authority of the administrative agency questioned? If so, use one of the following methods:

__ 1. Descriptive Word Method: Use the key words and phrases in the General Index of the constitutional volumes.
__ 2. Topic Method: Go to the volume on that subject and then use the specific Individual Subject Index. *Note:* There are no cross references in the codes which lead the researcher to the constitutional provision.

Do you have a case that interprets a constitutional provision and you want more cases on this point? If so, use one of the following methods:

__ 3. Look under the Index of Notes of Decision in the *U.S.C.A.* or *U.S.C.S.* for the constitutional provision you are researching and find the most appropriate note. Then check the bound volumes, pocket parts, and pamphlet supplements, if any.
__ 4. Obtain the topic and key number from the "one good case" and use it in the various federal digests.

The following example will demonstrate how a constitutional problem can be researched when a direct constitutional issue is involved.

EXAMPLE: The defendant was arrested at the Orlando International Airport for the possession of cocaine. After he had checked his baggage, a suspicious Drug Enforcement Agent had Zeke, a trained canine, examine one of the bags. Zeke immediately detected the presence of contraband. Having been convicted in the federal district court, the Defendant raises a constitutional error on appeal. The issue before the court of appeals is whether the use of dogs trained in drug detection constitutes a "search" under the United States Constitution.

[1] Topic Method

If the researcher has some familiarity with constitutional law, it is apparent that this is a search problem which is controlled by the Fourth Amendment. Thus, by using the Topic Method, the researcher would simply find the volumes in the *U.S.C.A.* or the *U.S.C.S.* that deal with the Fourth Amendment.

[2] Descriptive Word Method

The Descriptive Word Method is the most common starting point if the researcher simply has a fact situation but does not know what constitutional provision will provide the answer. This method requires a more thorough analysis of the problem. To analyze this issue, the researcher should use the TAPP rule which is commonly used for statutory analysis. TAPP is an acrostic for Things, Acts, Persons, and Places. Some of the words that might be used in our illustration might be:

Things:	search, trained dogs, luggage, baggage
Acts:	possession of cocaine, drugs, contraband
Persons:	Drug Enforcement Agency agent, traveler
Places:	airport

§ C FINDING AND UPDATING A CONSTITUTIONAL PROVISION

1. *Index Bound Volume:* Use the key words and phrases in one of the two indices. The first is the Constitutional Index which is at the end of the last constitutional volume. Under the phrase "searches and seizures," there is a reference to the Fourth Amendment. However, the Constitutional Index is a small index, and therefore, if the researcher has any difficulty in locating the provision, the eight volume General Index at the end of the statutory law code volumes can be consulted. Many words are listed under the term "searches and seizures" in that volume. Adding the subdivision "constitution," however, would also refer the researcher to the Fourth Amendment.

2. *Index Pocket Part:* Index information as well as all other materials must be updated in the pocket part of the bound volume. However, there are no new entries. If the researcher uses the General Index, there is no pocket part because it is published annually in a softbound cover. This softbound format has been used since the mid-1980's.

3. *Read and Analyze the Provision in the Bound Volume:* The researcher must read carefully the constitutional provision in the bound volume. In this case, the Fourth Amendment will be too general to answer the question. The Fourth Amendment simply states that people have the right "to be secure in their persons, houses, papers, and effects, against unreasonable searches and seizures . . . ." Thus, it is important to check for interpretive case law which has defined what constitutes a search. Part of the analysis process is to review the research aids to determine if there is any other relevant information. These aids might lead the researcher to helpful primary or secondary authority.

4. *Pocket Part:* Update the constitutional provision. Although as a practical matter the Constitution has not been amended recently, the researcher should follow the updating procedures. This should be done by reviewing the pocket

part in the back of the bound volume. In this problem, there are no changes or additions to the Fourth Amendment.

5. *Supplementary Pamphlet:* Sometimes a quarterly paper-bound supplement will be issued if there have been many new cases. If there are so many cases that this is impractical, then a bound volume may be issued. Therefore, the researcher should be aware of these possibilities and look for a supplementary pamphlet. In the present example, there is a 1999 supplementary pamphlet.

6. *Shepardize the Provision:* The final update would be to Shepardize the provision in *SHEPARD'S U.S. Citations,* statutes volumes. *SHEPARD'S* will update the constitutional provision itself by noting if there have been any amendments to it or if it has been repealed.

§ D   FINDING AND UPDATING INTERPRETIVE CASES

The next step in the research process is to find interpretive case law. This may be done in several ways. The most common method is outlined below:

1. *Bound Volume:* Following the research aids section is an Index for the Notes of Decision. Due to the large number of cases that have interpreted the Constitution, a general note index is listed by roman numerals. In addition, a more detailed alphabetical note index precedes each general area. Quick access to the relevant cases is provided through this Index. Thus, the researcher should scan the Index using the key words and phrases that were obtained through the TAPP rule analysis. For instance, the most appropriate general index heading for this problem is "XXIII. Conduct Constituting Search or Seizure." Turning to the more specific index and looking under "dog sniffing inspections" at note 1723, there are two on-point cases: *United States v. Place*, a United States Supreme Court decision, and *United States v. Goldstein*, an Eleventh Circuit Court of Appeals case from Florida. The most specific word in the analysis should be used. Merely using the word "dogs," the researcher will find that there is nothing directly on point in the bound volume.

2. *Pocket Part:* The pocket part should always be checked under the relevant note number.

3. *Pamphlet Supplement:* If a quarterly pamphlet has been published, then it should be checked by using the relevant note number.

   Although the researcher has found an on-point case, all the updating procedures need to be followed. *United States v.*

Place directly answers the question. It also demonstrates the research point that ultimately the researcher is looking for a United States Supreme Court case because it is the highest judicial authority.

4. *Shepardize:* The last important step in the research process is to read, analyze, and Shepardize any relevant case in the appropriate citator.

Computer Note

LEXIS-NEXIS has a separate database for the Constitution which is the CONST file in the states which have statutory materials on-line. For example, the researcher could find the Texas Constitution in the state library TXCNST. In the GENFED library, there is now a USCNST file to search the *U.S.C.S.* constitution volumes. For the text of the Constitution, a **WESTLAW** search would proceed through the statutory materials. To find the Constitution using relevant cases, use it as a search term. On the **Internet**, there are many sites where the United States Constitution can be found. The Government Printing Office maintains a site at <http://www.access.gpo.gov/congress/senate/constitution/index.html>.

The steps for researching a federal constitutional problem are summarized in the following checklist:

CONSTITUTIONAL LAW CHECKLIST

1. Analyze the facts according to the TAPP rule to determine the key words and phrases.

2. Find the appropriate constitutional provision in the *U.S.C.A.* or the *U.S.C.S.* by:

   a. the Topic Method; or,

   b. the Descriptive Word Method.

3. Read and analyze the appropriate constitutional provision in the bound volumes of the *U.S.C.A.* or the *U.S.C.S.*

4. Review the research aids to determine if there are cross references to other primary or secondary authorities.

5. Update the constitutional provision by:

   a. the annual pocket part;

   b. the quarterly pamphlet supplement, if any; and,

   c. *SHEPARD'S U.S. Citations*, statutes volume.

6. Find relevant interpretive case law by:

   a. the Notes of Decision in the *U.S.C.A.* or *U.S.C.S.* in the bound volume;

   b. the digests, if you already have "one good case"; or,

   c. secondary resources such as annotations, treatises, or law review articles if you do not know very much about the subject.

7. Update the case law by:

   a. the annual pocket part;

   b. the quarterly pamphlet supplement, if any; and,

   c. the appropriate *SHEPARD'S* citator.

8. Read, analyze, and Shepardize all cases.

Chapter 3

FEDERAL LEGISLATIVE RESEARCH

§ A FEDERAL LAW ORGANIZATION

Federal legislative materials are another source of primary authority. Because the common law emphasis has always centered on judicial opinions, the researcher has to fight the tendency to overlook legislation. This is especially true because a growing number of cases involve the interpretation of statutes. In fact, the careful researcher should always ask the following question before beginning any research assignment: Is there a relevant statute?

Researching federal statutes is a complex process because it involves finding and updating the statute. That process, however, is not enough by itself. A statute does not exist in a vacuum. Its validity depends in large part upon the way it is enforced or interpreted by the courts. Any research, then, that involves federal statutes necessarily includes the extra steps of finding interpretive cases. To understand this entire process, it is best to begin with the methods by which statutes are published officially and unofficially.

When the United States Congress passes legislation, it is published officially in three phases, as illustrated by the diagram below:

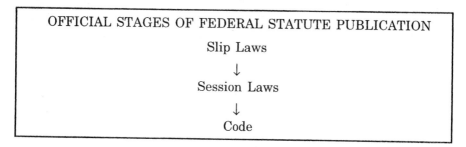

```
┌─────────────────────────────────────────────────────────┐
│   OFFICIAL STAGES OF FEDERAL STATUTE PUBLICATION          │
│                                                           │
│                      Slip Laws                            │
│                         ↓                                 │
│                    Session Laws                           │
│                         ↓                                 │
│                        Code                               │
└─────────────────────────────────────────────────────────┘
```

[1] Official Sources

The first official stage of publication is a "slip law," an individual pamphlet that contains the text of a single act, similar to a slip opinion. Each slip law is paginated separately and contains a brief summary of its legislative history after the text. Slip laws are issued by their public law number, for example, P.L. 98-128. The first part of the number tells the reader that the law was enacted during the 98th Congress, while the second part of the number represents its chronological sequence of enactment, i.e., the 128th law enacted in the 98th Congress. Slip laws are produced by the United States Government Printing Office and are available in print and electronically on the Internet.

The second official stage of federal statutory publication is the "session" laws, so designated because they are published at the end of each session of Congress in chronological order by public law number. Variously comprised of as many as six volumes, these materials are known as the *United States Statutes at Large.* Subject and title indices appear at the end of each volume. While slow in publication, this is the authoritative source of federal legislation or *positive law,* which means that the version published in the session laws is legal evidence of statutory language in all United States courts. The researcher would use the session laws only when there is a dispute over the language of the statute or when it is necessary to know what the statutory language was during a specific time. Furthermore, the researcher should be aware that any subsequent amendments to the statute will be published separately after the session in which it was passed. Therefore, the researcher will have to locate any amendments individually.

The third official stage of publication is in a code. The codification process groups all laws related by subject, includes subsequent amendments, and eliminates those laws which have been repealed. The *United States Code (U.S.C.)* is the official compilation of laws for the United States and is arranged in fifty titles. A new edition of the Code is issued every six years and supplemented annually with cumulative bound volumes. The Code includes the full text of the statute, followed by a parenthetical reference to the cite of that section in the *Statutes at Large.* There is a general index, a popular name table, and a tables volume which provides cross references to the public law number and the *Statutes at Large* citation. Like other official publications, the *U.S.C.* supplementation is slow. More important to the researcher, however, is the absence of any reference to cases interpreting federal statutes. For this reason alone, the researcher will find the unofficial sources of more value.

Computer Note

LEXIS-NEXIS and **WESTLAW** provide access to the U.S. Code and notes of interpretive decisions. Recently enacted statutes are also available on **LEXIS-NEXIS** and **WESTLAW**. Slip laws are available through the **Internet** at the Library of Congress website <http://thomas.loc.gov>. The Government Printing Office website offers access to the U.S. Code at <http://www.access.gpo.gov/su_docs/aces/aaces002.html>.

---

[2] Unofficial Sources

Since there is no unofficial publication of slip laws, the first stage of publication of unofficial materials occurs with session laws. The *United States Code Congressional and Administrative News (U.S.C.C.A.N.),* published by West, provides on a monthly basis the full text of bills enacted into public law during that time. Also included are selected legislative histories in the form of committee reports for important legislation. LEXIS Publishing provides a similar unofficial session law service entitled the *United States Code Service Advance Service*. These services for statutes are analogous to advance sheets for court reports.

The second stage of unofficial publication is in annotated versions of the *U.S.C.* There are two sets covering this material: The *United States Code Annotated (U.S.C.A.)*, published by West, and the *United States Code Service (U.S.C.S.)*, published by LEXIS Publishing. Both sets publish the language of the U.S. Code statutes, their effective date, and brief descriptions or annotations of cases interpreting the statutes. Historical references provide citations to the *Statutes at Large* for the law and any amendments, as well as legislative history information. These volumes also have similar update services in the form of annual pocket parts and pamphlet supplements. Because of these similarities, the research processes described below can be applied to either set.

§ B   FEDERAL LAW LOCATION METHODS

The methods of finding federal statutes are similar to those employed to locate cases, depending upon the information the researcher already has. The simplest method will be described first.

LOOKING FOR A STATUTE?

Do you have the statute's popular name? If so, use one of the following methods:

— 1. The Popular Name Table in the annotated codes.
— 2. *SHEPARD'S Acts and Cases by Popular Names*.

Do you have only the statute's public law number or the *Statutes at Large* volume and page number?

— 3. Check the tables volumes of the annotated codes where conversion charts list all public acts in chronological order by public law number, *Statutes at Large* reference, and the corresponding *U.S.C.* title and section numbers.

If you do *not* have any of the references listed above, use one of the following methods:

— 4. Descriptive Word Method: Use the annotated codes' General Index.
— 5. Topic Method: Select general topics from the fifty titles in the U.S. Code and go to that title's index.

---

[1]   Popular Name Method

Assume that the researcher has only the popular name of a statute and wants to locate the legislation. The simplest technique for finding the statute is to go to the Popular Name Table in the *U.S.C.A.* or *U.S.C.S.*, which lists only those federal statutes with popular names in alphabetical order. Here is an illustration.

EXAMPLE: Assume that the federal statute's popular name is the Pregnancy Discrimination Act. Employ the following steps:

1. *Bound Volume:* Go to the paperbound General Index volume of the *U.S.C.A.* or *U.S.C.S.* containing the Popular Name Table. Check by alphabetical designation of the first name listed. In this example, you would look under "P" for pregnancy.

2. *Statute Volume:* When you find the Pregnancy Discrimination Act in the Popular Name Table, the citation will refer you to Title 42 of the Code, Section 2000e. Look up the statute in the appropriate annotated code volume.

[2] *SHEPARD'S Acts and Cases by Popular Names*

Another set of books that lists state and federal statutes by name in alphabetical order is *SHEPARD'S Acts and Cases by Popular Names* referred to in Chapter 1. Like the Popular Name Tables, these volumes include only those federal and state statutes which have popular names. Using the same example just described for Popular Name Table research, find the Pregnancy Discrimination Act using the following steps:

1. *Bound Volume:* Find the bound volume to *SHEPARD'S Acts and Cases by Popular Names* and look in the front of the book under "Federal and State Statutes" cited by popular name. In this example, look under "P" for the Pregnancy Discrimination Act.

2. *Supplementary Pamphlet:* If the popular name of the act is not listed in the bound volume, check the supplementary pamphlet using the technique described above. There you will find the citation for the title and section of the *U.S.C.* where the act is located.

3. *Statute Volume:* When you find the Pregnancy Discrimination Act, the citation will tell you to go to Title 42 of the U.S. Code, Section 2000e. Look up the statute in the appropriate annotated code volume.

[3] Tables Method

A quick way to locate federal legislation involves the tables volumes of the *U.S.C.A.* and *U.S.C.S.* When the researcher knows the public law number or has only the *Statutes at Large* cite, the tables volumes in the annotated codes provide cross references to the *U.S.C.* Here is a problem that illustrates this process.

EXAMPLE: The researcher knows that the Public Law Number is 91-452 § 1102(a) and wants to find the U.S Code title and section. Use the following steps:

1. *Bound Volume:* Go to the tables volume in the *U.S.C.A.* or *U.S.C.S.* Public laws are listed there in numerical order by session of Congress. Locate the 91st Congress and then Public Law Number 91-452. The *Statutes at Large* cite and the *U.S.C.* title and section number will be listed there. For this problem, 18 U.S.C. §§ 841-848 are the appropriate title and sections.

2. *Cumulative Supplement:* Check any supplements to the bound volume.

There are two subject matter methods of finding a statute. One problem will be used to demonstrate both of these methods.

EXAMPLE: A worker stayed home for three days with her young child, who was suffering from an ear infection. She has heard of a law that allows unpaid leave to care for relatives with a serious health condition. The issue is whether a child's ear infection qualifies as a "serious health condition" within the statute's meaning.

[4] Topic Method

One way to find a federal statute is by the *topic method.* A list of the fifty titles in the *U.S.C.* is published in the front of each volume of the unofficial annotated codes. As soon as the researcher becomes familiar with the code's organization, it is possible to select the correct title by glancing through these topics. The topic method for locating federal statutes is simpler than using the same procedure to find cases because there are only fifty topics in the code, compared to 435 in the digests.

Since the issue is an employment problem, the researcher can immediately identify Title 29 as "Labor Code" by scanning the fifty titles of the code. Such an approach would eliminate the need to use the General Index and allow the researcher to proceed directly to the individual title index. Using the TAPP rule again, the researcher would seek the words "family and medical leave," and under that heading would be referred to the section of the title that deals with "serious health conditions." The remainder of the research and update process would be identical to that described below.

[5] Descriptive Word Method

The *descriptive word method,* once again, is the most common means of locating a federal statute when the researcher has a fact situation with no popular name or immediately obvious topic that relates to one of the fifty code titles. The process should begin with an analysis of the facts according to the TAPP rule.

Using the descriptive word method, analyze the facts according to the TAPP rule, which is the common form of analysis for legislative materials. Some words that might be used in this analysis are:

Things: child's illness, absences
Acts: discrimination, family and medical leave
Persons: employee
Places: workplace

1. *Index Bound Volume:* The researcher should go to the General Index of the *U.S.C.A.* or the *U.S.C.S.* In either index the phrases "child's illness" and "employee" are too specific to be helpful. By contrast, the words "workplace" and "discrimination" are too general to be useful. The words "family medical leave," however, will lead to the appropriate title and section.

2. *Index Pocket Part:* In the *U.S.C.A.* and *U.S.C.S.*, the General Index is paperbound so there will be no pocket part.

3. *Read and Analyze the Provision in the Bound Volume:* Title 29 Section 2611 contains the information needed to determine the nature of the child's serious health condition. Read the language of the statute carefully and make note of the historical material directly following its language. Included there will be the effective date of the statute. This is important because the researcher must be sure to locate the provision in effect at the time of the legal dispute. Subsequent changes in the law may not be pertinent to the dispute. Citations to legislative history will also be noted, as well as cross references to the publishers' other sources, such as encyclopedias and form books.

§ C   FINDING AND UPDATING A FEDERAL LAW

Once you have located the statute and determined its applicability to your fact situation, check to see if the statute is still current or if it has been amended or repealed. To determine whether the statute has been changed subsequent to its enactment, follow the steps below.

1. *Pocket Part:* Check the cumulative annual pocket part found at the back of the *U.S.C.A.* or *U.S.C.S.* bound volume by title and section number.

2. *Supplementary Pamphlet:* If there is a cumulative supplementary pamphlet, check for the relevant title and section number.

3. *Session Laws:* Consult the unofficial session laws. This will tell you whether there has been any change during the current legislative session. Both unofficial session law services have cumulative tables of code sections amended or repealed. Locate the most recent issue of the monthly publications and check the title and section number of the act.

4. *Shepardize:* Federal statutes should be Shepardized in a manner similar to cases. *SHEPARD'S U.S. Citations,*

statutes volumes, covers the *U.S.C.* by title and section number. Citations are given to cases that have ruled on or discussed the statute. Most important to this process are the capital letters "C" and "U" which may appear to the left of a case citation. These letters tell the researcher that the court has found the statute constitutional or unconstitutional. Be sure to check all volumes and supplements to *SHEPARD'S* where the statute may appear.

§ D   FINDING AND UPDATING INTERPRETIVE CASES

Once you have located and updated a statute, the next task is to find a case on point that interprets the statute. Judicial interpretations can be found in the following manner:

1. *Bound Volume:* Following the statutory language in the bound volume of the annotated codes are Notes of Decisions which describe in short paragraphs those cases interpreting the statute. These Notes of Decisions are organized under subject headings and paragraph numbers. To locate case law interpreting a child's serious health condition, consult relevant Notes of Decision.

2. *Pocket Part:* To locate more recent decisions, read the relevant Notes of Decisions located by the appropriate paragraph number in the pocket part to find a case on point.

3. *Supplementary Pamphlet:* Check each pamphlet update by the same process.

4. *Advance Sheets:* Go to the *Cumulative Table of Statutes Construed* in the latest advance sheets for West's *Supreme Court Reporter, Federal Reporter,* and *Federal Supplement.* These tables will cite federal cases interpreting the statute which have been published in the reporter system but which have not yet been included in either the pocket part or a supplementary pamphlet.

5. *Shepardize:* Relevant cases should be Shepardized in the *SHEPARD'S* corresponding to the reporter where the case is reported.

LEGISLATIVE RESEARCH CHECKLIST

1. Analyze the fact situation according to the TAPP rule.
2. Locate the relevant statute by using:
   a. the Popular Name Table in the annotated code's General Index;
   b. *SHEPARD'S Acts and Cases by Popular Names*;
   c. the tables volumes in the annotated codes for the conversion charts;
   d. the Descriptive Word Method in the General Index; or
   e. the Topic Method in the fifty titles of the Code.
3. Read the statute, looking for particular language and any reference to legislative history.
4. Update the statute itself by:
   a. the pocket part;
   b. the supplementary pamphlet;
   c. the unofficial session laws; and
   d. Shepardizing the statute in *SHEPARD'S U.S. Citations,* statutes volume.
5. Find interpretive cases:
   a. check the Notes of Decisions in the bound volume,
   b. check the Notes of Decisions in the pocket part;
   c. check the Notes of Decisions in the supplementary pamphlet;
   d. check the cumulative Tables of Statutes Construed in the advance sheets of all federal court reports; and
   e. Shepardize all relevant cases in the appropriate *SHEPARD'S.*

§ E FEDERAL LEGISLATIVE HISTORY

The legislative history of federal statutes can be important to the researcher for two main reasons. First, the status of pending legislation may need to be traced, or for laws already enacted, it may be necessary to determine the legislative intent of an act. Second, courts use legislative intent to determine the meaning of vague language in a statute, the reason for any change in a statute, or for a statement of the law's purpose. Because so many sources must be consulted, researching legislative history can be a very complex process. With the advent of certain unofficial sources, however, research into legislative history has become more straightforward.

A complete legislative history involves various elements related to the process by which a bill becomes law. As the detailed chart at the end of this section indicates, relevant information may be obtained at various levels of the legislative process. In addition, some elements of a legislative history carry more weight than others and are summarized briefly below in order of importance:

1. *Committee Reports.* These are the most important items of a legislative history. Issued when a bill is reported out of either House, Senate, or Conference Committee, committee reports often contain the bill itself, an analysis of its content and its purpose, any suggested changes, as well as the reasons for the committee's specific proposals. Minority reports, if any, are also included.

2. *Bills.* The proposed legislation itself is also important in a legislative history. When a bill is introduced into the House or Senate, it is assigned a number. This number identifies the bill within that particular chamber. If an identical bill is submitted to both houses, a separate number will be assigned by each chamber. The bill number remains the same for a session of Congress. If the bill does not pass by the end of the session, then it must be resubmitted in the next session, at which time new numbers will be assigned. A bill may be amended or changed at any time during the legislative process. Each change may be important to the history of the bill as a reflection of congressional intent.

3. *Congressional Debates.* Floor discussion of proposed legislation can occur at any time in the enactment process, although generally debates take place after a bill has been reported out of committee. These debates sometimes focus on the intent of Congress; however, because individual members of Congress can manipulate these proceedings in a manner calculated to sway a court's interpretation of legislative intent, the importance of congressional debates is reduced.

4. *Hearings.* Senate and House committees may hold hearings to study pending legislation. Such hearings usually include testimony from non-legislators, such as experts and concerned citizens. As a result, their importance for the purposes of determining legislative intent is reduced. Moreover, not all committee hearings are published.

Most elements of a legislative history are available through official sources. Committee Reports are numbered and published individually. These reports are listed in the *Monthly Catalog of U.S. Government Publications.* The reports are also published in a bound series of House and Senate documents called the *Serial Set.* Proposed bills are also published individually and may be obtained from Congress or from libraries that subscribe to a microfiche service or are designated federal depositories. Congressional debates are published in the *Congressional Record* and issued daily while Congress is in session. The daily issues are then cumulated into an annual bound volume. While the *Congressional Record* attempts to record debate verbatim, legislators may revise their remarks. These revisions appear in the Appendix for each daily issue but not in the annual bound volumes. The *Congressional Record* is indexed every two weeks by title of legislation, subject matter, and legislator's name. These indices are not, however, cumulated until the annual bound volume appears.

Unofficial publications also provide access to the elements of a legislative history. A good starting point is Johnson's *Sources of Compiled Legislative History*, which lists major compilations of legislative history by publisher, subject matter, and public law number. The Congressional Information Service (C.I.S.) is the unofficial source that provides the most complete coverage in one set of legislative history sources. Commenced in 1970, this service issues a monthly index of committee reports, hearings and documents. These indices are cumulated quarterly and annually. Another good feature of this service is the abstracts provided for these materials. There is also a status table for pending legislation. The annual bound volumes provide the most important element to the researcher — cumulative legislative history of all laws passed. Since the mid-1980's, a separate, annual legislative history volume appears, arranged in chronological order by public law number. To coordinate with the indices, C.I.S. has instituted a microfiche service, also begun in 1970, offering the full text of all documents in the index volumes.

Another unofficial publication that provides quick access to the status of pending legislation is the *Congressional Index* published by Commerce Clearing House. Issued in two volumes, the set provides tables arranged by subject matter, sponsors' names, and status tables, with references to hearings and committee reports. Updated weekly, the service is an excellent reference to locate quickly a bill's status. The set, however, does not provide the text of committee reports, bills, hearings, or debates.

An unofficial source of more limited use is *U.S.C.C.A.N,*, which selectively publishes some committee reports, as well as a legislative history table of laws enacted. Pending legislation, however, is omitted and no abstracts are provided.

LOOKING FOR FEDERAL LEGISLATIVE HISTORY?

Do you need the status of pending legislation? If so, use the following method:

— 1. *Congressional Index* status table: Arranged by House or Senate bill number.

Do you need the legislative history of a statute already enacted? If so, use the following method:

— 2. C.I.S. annual legislative history volumes: Check the legislative history arranged by public law number.

---

[1] Legislative History of Pending Legislation

The *Congressional Index* status table is updated weekly and provides information on pending legislation. Here is an illustration:

EXAMPLE: The researcher wants to know the status of a bill pending in the Senate regarding an increase in the amount of leave time for federal employees who are organ donors.

1. *Subject Index:* Find the bill number in Volume 2 by looking in the Subject Index. A House or Senate Bill number, if any, will be listed there.

2. *Status Table:* There is a separate status table for House and Senate bills, arranged in chronological order by bill number. Check the appropriate table accordingly.

Computer Note

The full text of congressional bills is available on **LEXIS-NEXIS** and **WESTLAW**. The Government Printing Office website publishes bills at <http://www.access.gpo.gov/su_docs/aces/aaces002.html>.

---

[2] Legislative History of Federal Statutes

Assume that the statute has already been enacted and the researcher has the public law number and date of passage. Below is a problem to illustrate the process.

EXAMPLE: While researching the family leave problem earlier in the chapter, you notice a reference to Senate Report 103-3. The public law number is 103-3, which you found in the legislative history notes of the *U.S.C.A.* or *U.S.C.S.* volume where the statute is published. Use the following steps:

1. With the public law number, go to the C.I.S. Annual Legislative History Volume for 1993 and locate Public Law No. 103-3 where the Senate Report will be listed.

2. There you will find a brief synopsis of the statute, as well as a complete list of the documents in the legislative history, with references to reports, hearings, and debates.

3. Copies of the law itself, the reports, and hearings can be obtained through the C.I.S. microfiche collection or individually through official sources. Debate material must be located directly from the *Congressional Record*.

FEDERAL LEGISLATIVE HISTORY CHECKLIST

1. Analyze the fact situation to determine whether you need the status of pending legislation or the history of a law already passed.

2. Locate the relevant material for pending legislation by using *Congressional Index* by Commerce Clearing House.

3. Find legislative history of a law already passed by:

   a. checking the legislative history notes in *U.S.C.A.* or *U.S.C.S.*, following the language of the statute. Note the date the change was made and the public law number;

   b. checking appropriate annual C.I.S. Abstracts volume or, since 1984, legislative history volume section or legislative history components; and

   c. obtaining all documents listed from C.I.S. microfiche, if available or, if not, from official sources such as the *Congressional Record*.

FEDERAL LEGISLATIVE HISTORY CHART

Legislative Process	Possible Documents	How to Find
1. Preliminary Matters	Hearings may be held prior to the introduction of a bill on a problem. The problem may be discussed during several Congressional sessions.	Locate through: a. Monthly Catalog of U.S. Gov't Publications; or, b. C.I.S.
2. Presidential Statements	Presidential message or a memo from an executive agency. These reveal the purpose of the legislation and the intent of the drafters. Example: President's State of the Union Address.	Printed in: a. *Congressional Record*, b. *Weekly Compilation of Presidential Documents;* c. House & Senate Journals; or, d. House & Senate Documents.
3. Bill is introduced	Amendments to the bill are helpful in determining legislative intent. Likewise, the inclusion or deletion of particular language aids in determining legislative intent.	Available: a. on microfiche at libraries that subscribe to a microfiche service or are a federal depository; or, b. C.I.S. microfiche service beginning with the 89th Congress.
4. Referred to a Committee	Committee prints of the bill.	Available on an individual basis.
5. Hearings	May be held to investigate the problem and to elicit the views of individuals or groups who may be expert or lay witnesses. May publish a transcript of testimony and exhibits. Criticized because it contains the views of non-legislators. But it is helpful because it contains information regarding *why* Congress adopted or rejected certain language.	Locate through: a. Monthly Catalog of U.S. Gov't Publications; b. CCH *Congressional Index;* c. U.S. Senate Publication (Gov't Printing Office); d. C.I.S.; or, e. the *Cumulative Index of Congressional Hearings*, published by the Library of the U.S. Senate and dating back to the 41st Congress. Available through the Gov't Printing Office.
6. Committee Reports	This is one of the most valuable sources because they contain an analysis of the bill's content and intent, the committee's recommendations and reasoning, minority report, etc.	Available: a. individual pamphlets by report number; b. House & Senate Documents, "Serial Set"; c. Listed in the Monthly Catalog of U.S. Gov't Publications.

FEDERAL LEGISLATIVE HISTORY CHART

Legislative Process	Possible Documents	How to Find
7. Congressional Debates	Arguments for or against the bill or amendments are made or explanations of unclear portions may be stated. This source of legislative history has been criticized.	May be found in the *Congressional Record*.
8. Final vote	An "engrossed bill," the final draft copy, is presented for vote.	Action is recorded in the *Congressional Record*.
9. Sent to other house	Generally the same procedure as #4 through #8.	Generally the same documents and publications as #4 through #8.
10. Referred to a Conference Committee	If the House & Senate bills do not contain the same language, then a conference committee will review them to try and reconcile any differences. A conference report may be issued.	Published the same as a committee report described in #6.
11. Passage by the second house	An "enrolled bill," one that is signed by the Speaker of the House or the President of the Senate, is sent to the President.	This is generally not available to the public.
12. Presidential action	The President may veto or approve the bill and include a statement as to his reasoning.	Available through: a. Presidential Message may exist as to the approval or veto; or, b. Legislative History information may by noted in the publication process, *i.e.*, *U.S.C.C.A.N.*, *Statutes at Large*, and the codes.

Computer Note

LEXIS-NEXIS and **WESTLAW** provide access to selected Committee Reports, as well as the Congressional Record (since 1985). **Internet** access to Committee Reports and the Congressional Record is available through the Government Printing Office website, as well as the C.I.S. website by subscription.

Chapter 4

FEDERAL ADMINISTRATIVE RESEARCH

§ A ADMINISTRATIVE LAW ORGANIZATION

The administrative function of the federal government has by tradition been relegated to a status below that of judicial decisions and federal statutes. This is due in large measure to the fact that the agencies responsible for administering federal laws derive their authority through delegation of power from either the President or Congress. However, the growth of federal authority, in the form of increasingly complex federal statutes and executive functions, has made it necessary for anyone doing legal research to understand that whenever specific implementation of the law is at issue, it is necessary to find and update all relevant administrative materials.

These materials take many forms, depending upon their purpose. The President's office, for example, issues executive orders and proclamations that affect the function and organization of administrative agencies. Those agencies issue licenses, orders, opinions, decisions, and, probably most important, rules and regulations that articulate the means by which federal laws are enforced. Because federal rules and regulations generally have the greatest impact of all administrative functions, this chapter will focus on the complex process of how they are published and updated. Like federal statutes, these rules and regulations do not exist in a vacuum, and their enforcement depends upon the federal courts and administrative agencies for interpretation. All research into federal rules and regulations will, as a result, include the extra steps of finding any interpretive cases. To explain this process, it is best to begin with the official method by which federal rules and regulations are published.

[1] Official Sources

In order for any federal rule or regulation to take effect, it must first be published in the *Federal Register*. Produced by the Government Printing Office, the *Federal Register* is issued daily except for Saturday, Sunday, and holidays. Analogous to the *United States Statutes at Large,* it contains rules and regulations arranged by the title and part numbers of the *Code of Federal Regulations (C.F.R.)*, which will be discussed below. Each issue of the *Federal Register* contains an index of that day's changes in rules and regulations, as well as a cumulative list of all changes from the beginning of the month forward to that day. At the end of each month a separate pamphlet index appears, followed ultimately by an annual index.

After a rule or regulation appears in the *Federal Register*, it is incorporated into the *C.F.R.*, arranged in fifty titles similar, but not identical to, the *U.S.C.* Each title is divided into chapters which usually bear the name of the issuing agency. Each chapter is further subdivided into parts covering specific regulatory areas. An index, issued annually, is contained in a separate volume entitled *C.F.R. Index and Finding Aids*, which has been criticized as too general in its classification of subject terms. Published annually, the *C.F.R.* is issued at quarterly intervals as follows:

Titles 1 through 16 published as of 1/1

Titles 17 through 27 published as of 4/1

Titles 28 through 41 published as of 7/1

Titles 42 through 50 published as of 10/1

Each title contains all regulations still in force, incorporating those that took effect during the preceding twelve months and deleting those revoked.

An official guide to the organization of federal agencies is produced by the Office of the Federal Register and entitled the *United States Government Manual*. Issued annually, it explains how agencies function and provides names and addresses of Washington and regional offices. Thus, it can be a useful starting point if the researcher does not know anything about the relevant agency.

Computer Note

The National Archives and Records Association makes the U.S. Government Manual available on the **Internet** at <http:/// www.access.gpo.gov/nara/nara011.html>.

---

[2] Unofficial Sources

There is no unofficial source that prints all federal rules and regulations. There are, however, several unofficial sources that provide index services for the *Federal Register* and the *C.F.R.*

The Congressional Information Service (C.I.S.) publishes a weekly index for the *Federal Register* entitled the *Federal Register Index,* which organizes material by subject and by name, if the rule or regulation has a specific name. It also includes an index by *C.F.R.* title and part number.

For unofficial access into the *C.F.R.*, C.I.S. also publishes a four-volume annual *Index to the Code of Federal Regulations*. It provides a detailed subject index, as well as a geographic index. Its publication, however, is slow. The *U.S.C.S.* includes a paperbound one-volume reprint of the *C.F.R. Index* as part of the *U.S.C.S.* materials.

In addition, unofficial looseleaf services provide access to specific rules and regulations of individual agencies, such as the *Employment Practices Guide* by Commerce Clearing House.

Computer Note

LEXIS-NEXIS and **WESTLAW** provide access to the *Federal Register* and the *C.F.R.* **Internet** access to both the *Federal Register* and the *C.F.R.* is provided at the Government Printing Office website.

---

§ B FEDERAL RULE AND REGULATION LOCATION METHODS

The methods of finding federal rules and regulations are similar to those used to locate federal statutes, depending on what information the researcher possesses. The simplest method will be described first.

LOOKING FOR A FEDERAL RULE OR REGULATION?

Do you have the enabling legislation? If so, use the following method:

— 1. *C.F.R. Index and Finding Aids* volume: Lists federal statutes in the Parallel Table of Authorities by title and section numbers matched with the title and part numbers to corresponding rules and regulations.

If you do not have the enabling legislation, use one of the following methods:

— 2. Descriptive Word Method: Information arranged according to subject matter in the *C.F.R. Index and Finding Aids* volume.
— 3. Topic Method: Information arranged according to the fifty topics or titles in the *C.F.R.*
— 4. Agency Method: Agencies arranged in alphabetical order in the *C.F.R. Index and Finding Aids* volume.

---

[1] Enabling Legislation Method

Assume that the researcher only has the enabling legislation, *i.e.*, the federal statute that gives the agency issuing the rule or regulation its authority to do so. The simplest technique for finding the rule or regulation is to go to the most recent annual index in the *C.F.R.* and check the Parallel Table of Authorities. Here is an illustration:

EXAMPLE: Assume that you need to locate any federal rules and regulations derived from the family leave statute researched in the chapter on federal legislation. You have only the title and section number of the statute authorizing these regulations, in this instance 29 U.S.C. § 2654. Use the following steps:

1. *Index Volume:* Go to the annual *C.F.R. Index and Finding Aids* volume and locate the parallel table of authorities. This table provides cross reference by U.S. Code title and

section number, listed in chronological order, into any applicable *C.F.R.* title and section number.

2. *Bound Volume:* When you check the Parallel Table of Authorities under title 29, section 2654, there will be a reference to 29 C.F.R. § 825 *et seq.* Go to that title and read the regulations.

[2] Descriptive Word Method

The most common means of locating a federal rule or regulation is the descriptive word method. In analyzing the facts, the researcher should pay particular attention to the date of the dispute. The rule or regulation in effect at the time that the legal dispute arose must be located. This means that if a 1993 rule or regulation is at issue, the researcher would begin the descriptive word process in the index for that year. Here is a problem that illustrates this process:

EXAMPLE: Ann Alergie took a flight from Illinois to Florida on a commercial air carrier. During the flight, she smelled tobacco smoke in the forward lavatory and reported it to a flight attendant. Even though the smoke alarm went off, nothing was done. Ann Alergie wants to know whether smoking in a lavatory violates a federal rule.

Using the TAPP rule, the reader might employ the following words or phrases:

Things:	tobacco or cigarettes
Acts:	smoking
Persons:	passengers
Places:	aircraft

The researcher should go to the current annual index of the *C.F.R.* issued in soft cover. There are no entries under "tobacco" pertaining to airline flights, and no entries for "passengers". "Smoking" lists a provision for "Aircraft, smoking aboard," and "cigarettes" refers back to "smoking." Thus, the applicable provision appears to be that listed under "Smoking" with the subheading "Aircraft, smoking aboard."

Once the researcher has located the appropriate title and part number in the index volume, the next step is to go to the appropriate title and part in the *C.F.R.* Title 14, Aeronautics and Space, appears in the annual paperbound volume issued on January 1. Read through part 252. Note there the cross reference to the enabling legislation that provides the authority for these rules and regulations.

[3] Topic Method

A less reliable way to find a federal rule or regulation is the topic method. If the researcher is familiar with the fifty titles in the *C.F.R.*, it is possible to select the correct topic by glancing through each title's subject.

The same smoking issue may be used to demonstrate the topic method. Because the issue centers around smoking on aircraft, the most obvious choice would be title 14, "Aeronautics and Space." This title provides the rules and regulations governing the aircraft. A complicating factor is the absence of individual indices within each title, which forces the reader to scan all subdivisions of every topic, often spanning several volumes, to locate the relevant part. If the researcher nevertheless were to locate the appropriate provision, the remainder of the research and update process set out below would be identical to that used with the descriptive word method.

[4] Agency Method

The *C.F.R. Index and Finding Aids* volume lists agencies and where materials for a specific agency can be found. That section of the Index is entitled "Alphabetical List of Agencies Appearing in the C.F.R." Because the references are to a general code title, this method is used if the researcher is looking for the agency's body of regulations or wants to combine this method with the topic method.

§ C UPDATING FEDERAL RULES AND REGULATIONS

Once you have located and read the rule or regulation applicable to the problem, the next step is to determine whether any changes have occurred since the publication date listed on the cover of the *C.F.R.* volume. Follow the steps below:

1. *Supplementary Pamphlet:* Check the most recent issue of the monthly *C.F.R. List of Sections Affected (L.S.A.).* Arranged by title and section number, this publication will cite to a page in the *Federal Register* if any change has occurred to Title 14, Part 252.

2. *Federal Register:* Locate the most recent issue of the daily *Federal Register.* At the end of each issue is a cumulative list of sections affected for the month arranged by title and part number. If a change has occurred, its page number in the *Federal Register* is given. Because the *Federal Register* is published and distributed so quickly, you should be able to update with this source to some time within a week of the current date.

§ D FINDING AND UPDATING INTERPRETIVE CASES

Once you have located and updated a federal rule or regulation, there are four ways of finding interpretive cases:

1. *SHEPARD'S:* Federal rules and regulations should be Shepardized in a manner similar to federal statutes, *i.e.,* by title and part number. The purpose of Shepardizing a

rule or regulation is to locate interpretive cases, since case annotations are lacking in both the *C.F.R.* and the *Federal Register. SHEPARD'S Code of Federal Regulations Citations* is a source for finding judicial treatment of federal rules and regulations. It does not, however, indicate whether an agency has repealed or deleted a rule or regulation. Be sure to check all volumes and supplements to the *SHEPARD'S C.F.R. Citations.*

2. *Federal Agency Publications:* At least thirty federal agencies render and publish official opinions. Because these decisions are issued in official reports, publication is slow. For a list of those agencies issuing official reports of their decisions, the researcher should consult the *Monthly Catalog of Government Publications.* Major agency decisions can be Shepardized in *SHEPARD'S United States Administrative Citations. SHEPARD'S* also publishes separate citators for some administrative agency decisions, for example, *Federal Labor Law Citations* and *Federal Energy Law Citations.*

3. *Unofficial Reporters:* There is no single source that publishes decisions from all administrative agencies or all judicial interpretations of federal rules and regulations. There are, however, unofficial reports focusing on specific subject areas. For example, looseleaf services, such as the Bureau of National Affairs *Labor Relations Reference Manual*, offer coverage of agency and federal court decisions, as well as frequent updates. Some of these unofficial sets provide their own citators. Otherwise, these cases should be Shepardized in the appropriate sets for federal cases, *United States Administrative Citations* for agency decisions, or *SHEPARD'S* subject oriented citators in the regulatory area.

Computer Note

LEXIS-NEXIS and **WESTLAW** have topical databases that include judicial and agency decisions.

FEDERAL RULES AND REGULATIONS CHECKLIST

1. Analyze the fact situation according to the TAPP rule.
2. Locate the relevant rule or regulation by using:
    a. the Parallel Table of Authorities in the *C.F.R. Index and Finding Aids* volume;
    b. the Descriptive Word Method in the same volume;
    c. the Topic Method; or,
    d. the Agency Method.
3. Read and analyze the rule or regulation.
4. Update the rule or regulation through:
    a. the monthly *C.F.R. List of Sections Affected*; and,
    b. the most recent daily *Federal Register* cumulative list of sections affected.
5. Find interpretive cases by:
    a. *SHEPARD'S C.F.R. Citations* for federal court decisions;
    b. federal agency publications for federal agency decisions; or,
    c. unofficial reporters for both agency and federal court decisions.
6. Update the judicial or agency decision by:
    a. the appropriate *SHEPARD'S* for judicial decisions;
    b. *SHEPARD'S United States Administrative Citations* for agency decisions; or,
    c. the relevant subject oriented citator.

Chapter 5

STATE CONSTITUTIONAL LAW RESEARCH

§ A STATE CONSTITUTIONAL ORGANIZATION

Each state has its own constitution which is generally patterned after the United States Constitution. However, the length or scope of these state constitutions will vary. Some, like the federal Constitution, are relatively brief while others are so voluminous that they include materials which probably should be contained in statutes.

The number of constitutional amendments will also vary. The state constitutions have been amended more frequently than the federal Constitution. Generally, these changes occur at a significant time in the state's history. For example, several revisions of the Texas Constitution coincided with critical periods in the state's political history. Some examples include:

(1) 1836: The new republic adopted a constitution which bore a strong resemblance to the U.S. Constitution in its separation of powers provision and its bill of rights.

(2) 1845: Introduced the change from the status of a republic to that of a state.

(3) 1861: Effected the withdrawal from the Union and a change to the Confederacy.

(4) 1869: Effected the readmittance to the Union.

(5) 1876: The present Constitution. It is long and verbose and has been subject to many amendments.

It is important for the researcher to determine if there is a constitutional provision on point. This is particularly significant when a legislative issue is involved because the constitution gives the legislature power to act. As indicated in the discussion of the federal Constitution, legislative material is based on a hierarchy of law. The constitution is the highest authority of the state and becomes the first tier of legislative materials. State constitutions also enumerate certain powers to the state legislatures. These powers enable the legislatures to act by passing statutes. This form of legislation is the second tier of authority. In addition, the state legislatures have authority to create state administrative agencies which fashion the day-to-day rules and regulations to implement the statutes. These administrative rules and regulations become the third tier of authority.

HIERARCHY OF AUTHORITY

State Constitution

↓

State Statutes

↓

State Administrative Rules and Regulations

The forms of publication are also similar to federal materials. In other words, there may be an official and unofficial publication of the constitution. At the present time, there are five states which have an official publication. These editions are printed by the State Legislative Council and may be the sole publication of the material within the state. However, the format and the research process for both the official and unofficial publication of a state constitution is basically the same. Once the researcher is familiar with the process, it is simply a matter of looking for that information to complete the research. For example, even the official publication of the code is annotated so that a case can be found. However, in two states, Nevada and Oregon, the annotations are not with the statutory provision but instead are found in separate binders.

As with other types of research, judicial interpretation of the state constitution is important. The annotated code is the most efficient way to find case authority for the constitutional material. However, alternate methods of both finding cases and updating the information are available. For example, the researcher can use the state digest under the appropriate topic and key number. In addition, the state edition of *SHEPARD'S*, statutes volumes, provides not only updating information about the constitutional provision but also any cases that have interpreted the section.

Another source of information is local secondary authority. For instance, state encyclopedias frequently contain historical information or references to such available materials. Furthermore, local treatises or law journal articles produced by practitioners, the state bar, or student authors may provide background information.

§ B STATE CONSTITUTIONAL LAW LOCATION METHODS

[1] State Code Method

Finding the text of the state constitution is a relatively easy matter. Each of the state statutory codes has the text of that state's constitution; this format is similar to federal research in the *U.S.C.A.* or the *U.S.C.S.* for the United States Constitution. Generally, the constitutional volumes precede the statutory volumes. For example, in Texas, the first four volumes of the *Vernon's Annotated Texas Code* contain the constitution.

In addition, both an official and unofficial state code will be annotated. This is important because of the impact of judicial decisions on constitutional law. Case law has two important functions. First, judicial opinions provide the necessary interpretation to constitutional provisions which by necessity have to be general in nature. Second, the case law analyzes and reviews the statutory language or acts of the parties to determine if they meet the template outlined in the constitution.

The format for research materials is generally the same. Slight variations may exist because of the differences between the many publishers of the state codes. However, these minor differences should not be a problem for the researcher. The constitutional provision will be divided according to articles. Following this major heading, a number of research aids are noted such as: (1) a "table of contents" of the sections within that article; (2) any notations about the article itself such as its title or if it has been amended or repealed; (3) a table of revised section numbers for each revision; (4) the text of the first section; (5) legislative changes to that section; (6) historical notes about the section; (7) a list of law journal articles about that section; (8) an index to the notes of decisions; and, (9) the listing of the cases.

[2] General Resources

Although the state code is the most commonly used method of finding a constitutional provision, there are other research tools available. The most notable is a multi-volume looseleaf set entitled *Constitutions of the United States: National and State* (2d ed. 1974) by Oceana Publications which contains the texts of the constitutions for all of the states. Because it uses a looseleaf format, it is kept current by frequent supplements. In 1980, a new and improved series of looseleaf indices, arranged according to subject matter, was introduced. As a companion text, the publisher has produced an *Index Digest of State Constitutions* which lists the subjects of constitutional provisions of the states in alphabetical order.

In addition, some states print pamphlets of the text. Due to lack of availability and the relatively small number of research aids that they contain, these are the least helpful resource tool.

[3] Historical Sources

Some legal research projects may require reviewing the provisions of prior constitutions or constitutional sections. As with current provisions, the best source of information is the state code.

Information from the constitutional conventions or drafters of the provision may prove to be a valuable research tool. Some state codes contain historical introductions to the constitution. In addition, the records, journals, proceedings, and other documents that may have been produced during the constitutional convention can be helpful.

LOOKING FOR A STATE CONSTITUTIONAL PROVISION?

Does the subject matter raise a constitutional issue; is there a statute that implements the Constitution; or is the authority of the administrative agency questioned? If so, use one of the following methods:

__ 1. Descriptive Word Method: Use the key words and phrases in the General Index of the constitutional volumes.

__ 2. Topic Method: Go to the volume on that subject and then use the specific Individual Subject Index.

__ 3. Cross References: In most state codes, there are cross references that lead the researcher to the constitutional provision.

Do you have a case that interprets a constitutional provision and you want more cases on this point? If so, locate as follows:

__ 4. Go to the constitutional provision and look under the Index of Notes of Decision to find the most appropriate note. Then check the bound volumes, pocket parts, and pamphlet supplements, if any.

__ 5. From the "one good case," obtain the topic and key number and use it in the various state digests.

The following example illustrates the process of locating information that relates to state constitutional law. The problem is one which raises a constitutional issue.

EXAMPLE: John Miller attends public school. The school district has a regulation that restricts the length that male students can wear their hair. John knows about the regulation but refuses to cut his hair. On January, 15, 1998, John was suspended from school for violating this regulation. He complains that this regulation violates the equal rights amendment to the Texas Constitution because it only applies to male students. Is the regulation unconstitutional under the equal rights amendment?

1. *The Topic Method.* If the researcher has some familiarity with constitutional law, it will be apparent that this is an equal rights problem. Therefore, by using the Topic Method, the researcher will go to the Index for the constitutional volumes and look under the topic of "equal rights." The Index will refer the researcher to "Generally, Art. 1, § 3." However, the more specific equal rights amendment follows the general provision and is noted as § 3a, "equality under the law."

2. *The Descriptive Word Method.* The researcher could also use the Descriptive Word Method to solve this problem.

This method should be used if the researcher is not as familiar with the topic area, and thus, a more thorough analysis of the problem is necessary. The first step in the research process would be to analyze the facts. Using the TAPP rule, the following analysis might be used:

Things: hair, hair length policy
Acts: discrimination, suspension, equality, equal rights
Persons: students, public schools, schools
Places: campus

§ C FINDING AND UPDATING A CONSTITUTIONAL PROVISION

1. *Index Bound Volume:* Use the key words and phrases in either the Index for the constitutional volumes or the General Index if it is more detailed. The key words for this problem are: schools, sex discrimination, and equal rights. These words would lead the researcher to Art. 1, § 3 of the Texas Constitution by looking under the "generally" section. However, as indicated, the more specific provision is Art. 1, § 3a.

2. *Index Pocket Part:* The index information as well as all other materials must be updated in the pocket part. The updated index of the Index for the Constitution volumes is located before the updated annotated text of the constitution in the pocket part. The General Index is published every two years in a softbound cover, and therefore, it has no pocket part.

3. *Read and Analyze the Provision in the Bound Volume:* The researcher must read carefully the constitutional provision in the bound volume. As the researcher will find, it is only a very general provision and does not specifically answer the question. It merely indicates that "equality under the law shall not be denied or abridged because of sex, race, color, creed, or national origin."

   Part of the analysis process is to review the research aids to determine if there is any other relevant information. For example, there are historical notes which indicate when the amendment became law, cross references to related statutory materials, a list of law journal articles on related subjects, library references to topic and key numbers in the digests, and related federal statutes and cases. These research aids should be scanned to see if there are any appropriate research tools.

4. *Pocket Part:* Update the constitutional provision. This should be done by reviewing the pocket part in the back

of the volume. In this problem, there are no changes or additions to the provision.

5. *Supplementary Pamphlet:* If any pamphlet supplements have been published on an interim basis, these pamphlets should be checked. In the present problem, there are no changes or additions to the provision.

6. *Shepardize the Provision:* The final update would be to Shepardize the provision in *SHEPARD'S Texas Citations,* statutes volume. This step would indicate if the provision has been amended or repealed.

§ D FINDING AND UPDATING INTERPRETIVE CASES

Once the researcher has located and updated the constitutional provision, it is important to find interpretive cases. Typically, the constitutional provision is general and vague, and therefore will not answer the researcher's specific question. Thus, interpretive cases or statutes will help the researcher answer the question. The following methods show you how to answer the legal question asked in the previous example by searching for judicial interpretation of the constitutional provision:

1. *Bound Volume:* Following the research aids is an Index for the Notes of Decision. Again, using the key words and phrases from the TAPP rule analysis, the most appropriate note for this problem is Note of Decision number fourteen. Under this note, there are two relevant cases: *Mercer v. Board of Trustees, North Forest ISD,* 538 S.W.2d 201 (Tex. Civ. App—Houston [14ᵗʰ Dist.] 1976) and *Toungate v. Board of Trustees of Bastrop ISD,* 842 S.W.2d 823 (Tex. App.— Austin 1992).

2. *Pocket Part:* The interpretive cases must also be updated. This should be done through the pocket part in the back of the volume by checking Note of Decision number fourteen. The researcher would find that the *Toungate* case was reversed and rendered in 958 S.W.2d 365 (Tex. 1997).

3. *Pamphlet Supplement:* Any pamphlet supplements that are available should be checked.

4. *Shepardize:* The actual opinions of the cases that will be used in a legal memorandum or appellate brief should be read and analyzed. Then they should be Shepardized in *SHEPARD'S Texas Citations,* case volume, if they are Texas cases.

In Texas, there is also another step in updating cases. The Subsequent History Table must be consulted to see if either the Texas Supreme Court (the court of last resort for civil cases) or the Texas Court of Criminal Appeals (the court of last resort for criminal cases) has agreed to review the case. There are three volumes that must be checked. They are: the green bound volume of the *Texas Subsequent History Table* (contains information for the last year); the advance sheets of the *Southwestern Reporter, Second Series*; Texas Cases (contain information within the last six weeks); and the *Texas Supreme Court Journal* (contains weekly information).

Computer Note

When the relevant state statutory materials are added to the databases, then the constitutional provisions are also added. Access on both **LEXIS-NEXIS** and **WESTLAW** is available through the statutory databases. On the **Internet**, the Texas Constitution can be found at <http://www.capitol.state.tx.us/txcon/toc.htm>.

STATE CONSTITUTIONAL CHECKLIST

1. Analyze the facts to determine the key words and phrases using:

    a. the Topic Method; or,

    b. the Descriptive Word Method.

2. Use the key words and phrases in the Index to the constitutional volumes of *Vernon's Annotated Texas Statutes* (*VATS*) or the General Index.

3. Read the relevant constitutional provision.

4. Review the research aids that follow the relevant section.

5. Update the constitutional provision by:

    a. the pocket part in the back of the bound volume;

    b. any pamphlet supplement; and,

    c. *SHEPARD'S Texas Citations*, statutes volume.

6. Find appropriate interpretive cases, if any, by:

    a. looking at the Index of Decisions for a specific Note of Decision; and,

    b. finding a pertinent Note of Decision number in the bound volumes, pocket parts, and possible pamphlet supplements.

7. Update the case law by:

    a. the pocket part in the back of the bound volume;

    b. any pamphlet supplement;

    c. reading and analyzing cases;

    d. *SHEPARD'S Texas Citations,* case volume; and,

    e. the Subsequent History Table of:

        (1) the bound volume;

        (2) the advance sheets of the *Southwestern Reporter, Second Series*, Texas Cases; and,

        (3) the *Texas Supreme Court Journal.*

Chapter 6

STATE LEGISLATIVE RESEARCH

§ A   STATE LAW ORGANIZATION

[1]   Overview

Most new law students read many state judicial opinions and often research such opinions as their first exposure to the ways of finding legal sources. As a consequence, there is a tendency to see all legal problems as a quest for common law decisions. Most practitioners, however, confront daily problems involving state statutes. Thus, finding these statutes and checking for any amendments becomes a routine task.

Because statutory language is often ambiguous, it is necessary to clarify its meaning. For example, in order to determine the purpose or intent of the legislature, the researcher would need to examine the legislative history of the act. Case law or State Attorney General Opinions that interpret the statute or its language would also be relevant. Finally, the rules or decisions by administrative agencies or boards might help the researcher to interpret the law as well. Thus, it is important for the researcher to recognize that legal research is an integrated process that requires different levels and types of research.

In addition, a statute in one state may be based on a similar federal or sister state statute. For example, the federal organized crime act (RICO) has been a template for many state statutes with only minor variances. Many states have adopted uniform laws prepared by the National Conference on Uniform State Laws. Therefore, if an act has a provision that is identical to a provision in another jurisdiction, interpretive case law from the sister jurisdiction may be persuasive authority.

[2]   Pattern of Publication

State statutory materials are published in the same pattern of publication as the federal statutory materials. Thus, a law is first published in the form of a slip law. At the end of the legislative session, the more commonly used session laws are published. The final form of publishing laws is in the codes and annotated codes. The following chart demonstrates the particular characteristics of each stage of publication. General statements are made about the publications and a specific state example is used.

STAGES OF PUBLICATION		
Form	**Generally**	**Specifically — Texas**
Slip Laws	1. Issued in most states. 2. Rarely used by the public.	1. No official publication.
Session Laws	1. Each state publishes a set that is similar to the Statutes at Large. 2. They are the authoritative text. 3. Generally, there are long delays in printing. 4. Non-cumulative indices.	1. Published on a regular basis under both the republic and state of Texas, *i.e.*, since 1941. West publishes the *General and Special Laws — Texas* in two volumes per year. 2. Same. 3. Same. However, there are unofficial advance services. For example *Vernon's Texas Session Law Service* (West); 4. Same.
Codes	1. Format is similar to the *U.S.C.* 2. Subject access. 3. Commercially published. 4. Generally unofficial. 5. Generally annotated. 6. Authority varies. 7. Supplemented — generally on an annual basis.	1. Same. 2. Same. 3. Published by West. 4. Unofficial. No official code since *Vernon's* in 1925. 5. Annotated. 6. Not authoritative. 7. Annual pocket parts and semi-annual pamphlets.

§ B STATE LAW LOCATION METHODS

Before the research process begins, you should examine the code to see how it is organized. Depending on your familiarity with the code, the subject matter, and the information available, you can use the popular name approach, topic method, or the descriptive word method to find the relevant provision.

LOOKING FOR A STATE STATUTE?

Do you have the popular name of the statute? If so, use the following methods:

— 1. Use the popular name table in the state code if one exists.
— 2. If one does not exist in the state code, then check *SHEPARD'S Acts and Cases by Popular Names.*

If you do not have the popular name of the statute, or if the statute does not have a popular name, use one of the following methods:

— 3. Topic Method: If familiar with the code, go directly to the relevant title.

Once in the appropriate title, scan the outline in front of the title to find the relevant chapter and section.

— 4. Descriptive Word Method: Use the key words and phrases from the TAPP rule analysis in the General Index.

The following example will demonstrate how a problem can be researched. Although this is a Texas problem, the research techniques can be used in any state code. The names of the publications may be slightly different; however, they will generally contain the same types of research materials.

EXAMPLE: A telephone lineman worked in a Texas coastal city facing threat of a hurricane. The governor ordered the city to evacuate, so the employee took his family inland for the storm's duration. When he returned to work he faced discharge for his absences during the storm. The issue is whether his discharge was wrongful when he obeyed an evacuation order.

[1] Popular Name Method

Unlike federal statutory sources, an annotated state code may not have a popular name table. Texas, however, has a popular name table in the paperbound General Index to the annotated state code. In addition, *SHEPARD'S Acts and Cases by Popular Names* lists both federal and state statutes by name; therefore, if there is a popular name, consult *SHEPARD'S.*

[2] Topic Method

Each code has an Individual Subject Index, often in the last volume of that subject. Thus, for example, the Probate Code has its own index and the Property Code has its individual index. If the researcher has a good working knowledge of the code and the subject matter, it is possible to make "an educated guess" as to where the statutory material will be located. It is then a matter of determining the key words and phrases for the problem, and then using those words in the volume containing the Individual Subject Index and its pocket part supplement.

[3] Descriptive Word Method

It is more likely that the researcher will have to use the descriptive word method. Therefore, the process should begin with analysis of the facts according to the TAPP rule. Then these key words and phrases would be used in the General Index for the state code.

The first step for solving this problem is to analyze the facts according to the TAPP rule. Some words that might be used in this analysis are:

Things:	emergency
Acts:	evacuation, discrimination
Persons:	employee, emergency personnel
Places:	vital services provider

§ C   FINDING AND UPDATING A STATE STATUTE

1. *Index Volume:* Use the key words for the problem in *Vernon's Annotated Texas Statutes* General Index. In this problem, the key words are "employees," "emergency," and "discrimination," leading to Labor Code 22.004 pertaining to employment discrimination for participation in emergency evacuation orders when the employee provides vital services. Although the *VATS* index is paperbound, be sure to check the pocket part of any hard cover index.

2. *Read and Analyze the Provision in the Bound Volume:* Once found, the statute should be read and analyzed. Part of the analysis is to review the research aids that follow the relevant section. In this case, there are none. However, in most cases, language regarding the effective date of the legislation should be checked to make sure that this act was in effect at the time that the problem arose. Furthermore, legislative history could be important depending on the particular problem and the information that is needed. A later section of this chapter discusses legislative history in more detail.

3. *Pocket Part:* Update the statutory provision in the annual pocket part. The researcher should check the annual pocket part in the back of the bound volume under the title and section number of the statute.

4. *Supplementary Pamphlet:* Depending on the amount of material that is available since the pocket part was issued, there might be a semi-annual pamphlet supplement. If one exists, then it should also be consulted by looking under the title and section number of the statute.

5. *Session Law Service:* Statutes are also updated by a session law service which update acts on a regular basis. Thus, the latest issue of *Vernon's Texas Session Law Service* should be checked.

6. *Shepardize the Provision:* Finally, SHEPARD'S *Texas Citations,* statutes volume, should also be used. These volumes will indicate whether the statute has been repealed or amended.

§ D FINDING AND UPDATING INTERPRETIVE CASES

The next step in the research process is to find interpretive case law. These cases will interpret specific statutory language, as well as determine whether a provision is either constitutional or valid. The method for finding interpretive case law is as follows:

1. *Bound Volume:* Use the key words and phrases in the Index to the Notes of Decisions to find the most appropriate Note for relevant cases, if any.

2. *Pocket Part:* Check the annual pocket part supplement in the back of the bound volume.

3. *Pamphlet Supplement:* In Texas, pamphlet supplements are issued on a semi-annual basis. If these pamphlet supplements exist, they should be checked.

4. *Advance Sheets:* More current case updates can be checked in the advance sheets of the regional reporter, e.g., *Southwestern Reporter, Second Series,* Texas Cases. These advance sheets contain a section entitled "Statutes Construed" Table. This table lists the recent cases that have interpreted statutory provisions.

5. *Shepardize:* SHEPARD'S *Texas Citations,* case volumes, should be used to verify and update the status of the case.

Finally, in Texas, the annual paperbound Subsequent History Table should be consulted to determine if any petitions have been issued by a court of last resort. Updates can be found in the advance sheets of the *Southwestern Reporter,* Texas Cases (printed weekly, but cases are three to six weeks old), and the *Texas Supreme Court Journal* (updated weekly). Not all states have a process analogous to the Subsequent History Table.

STATE STATUTORY CHECKLIST

1. Analyze the facts according to the TAPP rule.
2. Find the appropriate statute by:
   a. Popular Name in:
      (1) the Popular Name Table, if it exists, in the state code index for Texas, *VATS;* or,
      (2) *SHEPARD'S Acts and Cases by Popular Names;*
   b. Topic Method: Use the Individual Subject Index; or,
   c. Descriptive Word Method: Use the General Index.
3. Read the relevant statutory provision in the bound volume.
4. Review the research aids that follow the relevant section.
5. Update the statutory provision by:
   a. the pocket part supplement (annual);
   b. any pamphlet supplements (semi-annual);
   c. a session law service (monthly); and,
   d. *SHEPARD'S Citations,* statutes volumes, for relevant jurisdiction.
6. Find interpretive case law by:
   a. the Index to the Notes of Decision; and,
   b. the appropriate Note of Decision number in the bound volume.
7. Update the case law by:
   a. the pocket part supplement (annual);
   b. any pamphlet supplements (semi-annual);
   c. the advance sheets of the regional reporter, state cases volumes, Statutes Construed Table;
   d. *SHEPARD'S Texas Citations,* case volume; and,
   e. the Texas Subsequent History Table in:
      (1) the annual paperbound volume;
      (2) the advance sheets, *Southwestern Reporter,* Texas Cases (weekly, although cases are three to six weeks old); and,
      (3) the *Texas Supreme Court Journal* (weekly).

Computer Note

LEXIS-NEXIS and **WESTLAW** provide access to all state codes. **LEXIS-NEXIS** annotates all but two state codes and **WESTLAW** annotates all state codes. **Internet** access to state codes may be available at state websites.

§ E STATE LEGISLATIVE HISTORY

[1] Overview

The purpose of locating state legislative history is the same as that at the federal level — to determine the legislature's intent or to analyze any language changes in the statute. These legislative histories also include the same types of material as those at the federal level, such as committee reports, copies of the proposed bills and any amendments, committee hearings, and floor debates.

Finding legislative history at the federal level is a relatively easy matter compared to locating state legislative history, because what is available will vary greatly between the states. Generally, the legislatures will not publish their debates, committee reports, or hearings. Sometimes, a state legislature will tape this information and a transcript of the tape can be obtained. In Texas, the most accessible official documents are the Senate and House Journals. However, the problem with these research tools is that the Journals only contain brief minutes of the proceedings and the final vote on the legislation. Individual state research manuals, such as *The Texas Legislative Reference Manual* produced by the Legislative Reference Library, as well as its website, are good starting points. An excellent resource for determining what is available in the states is M. Fisher, *Guide to State Legislative and Administrative Materials,* 4th ed.

[2] Locating Legislative History

Finding state legislative history can be a problem. The first source the researcher should check is the state code. Under the research aids, it is possible to get some idea as to any documents that might exist. A second source might be a state legal research guide, if one is published. Finally, a librarian with extensive experience in state materials can be an invaluable aid.

A sample legislative history problem is omitted for lack of legislative sources, but as an example of the types of things that may be available at the state and federal level, the following chart shows the research steps that can be used. Texas materials are used as an example of state legislative history; however, what is available will vary from state-to-state as previously indicated.

LEGISLATIVE HISTORY CHECKLIST	
Federal	**Texas**
1. Discover what language interests you and when this language was added, amended, or repealed.	1. Same.
2. Determine what legislative history is available by: a. Checking the annotated code b. Using a commercial publication such as Johnson, *Sources of Compiled Legislative History Laws*	2. Same.
3. Go to the research finding tools such as: a. C.I.S. — since 1970 b. *U.S.C.C.A.N.* — has only selected histories c. *CCH Congressional Index*	3. Same. a. Legislative Reference Library in Austin b. State Archives c. House and Senate Journals d. Texas Register e. Legislative Intent Research Firms
4. Find the appropriate sources of legislative history: a. Primary sources: (1) Public law (2) Bills and amendments (3) Committee reports (4) Debates (5) Committee hearings (6) Presidential Messages, etc. (7) Attorney General Opinions b. Secondary sources: (1) Newspaper clippings (2) Law review articles	4. Same. a. Primary sources: (1) Statutes (2) Original bill files for fiscal notes and analysis (3) Committee minutes (4) Debates (5) Hearings (6) Governor's Messages (7) Attorney General Opinions b. Secondary sources: (1) Newspaper clippings (2) Law review articles (3) Legislative clipping service (4) "Accomplishments of the Legislature"

§ F MUNICIPAL LEGISLATION

[1] Municipal Law Organization

Local governments, such as cities and counties, are usually called municipal corporations. As a general rule, they obtain their power from the state. Thus, if the research problem involves a question of the city or county's authority to act, the state constitution or statutes must be examined.

There are two kinds of legislative materials that are available at the local level. The first is the charter of the municipal corporation. It is analogous to the state constitution. In larger cities, the municipal charter generally is published in the same volumes that contain the city code. However, in smaller cities, the form of publication may vary. In some cities there is no accessible, up-to-date compilation of legislative materials. Thus, city charters would have to be obtained from the city or county clerk's office. A growing number of cities, however, provide access to their charters through a home page.

The second type of legislation is an ordinance. Ordinances, analogous to state statutes, are enacted by the local governing body such as the city council. The publication of ordinances will also vary according to the size of the city. For example, they may be printed in the city code, an official journal of the governing body, in slip form, or in the local newspaper. Like city charters, municipal ordinances are now increasingly available at a city's website.

[2] Municipal Law Location Methods

The most common method of researching a city charter or ordinance is through the city code. However, if an ordinance has not been codified, copies of it may be obtained through the city clerk's office. City codes are similar to the state codes in that they contain the text of the ordinance or charter, topical analysis, historical notes, cross references, indices, and tables of the location of earlier sections in the new code.

Another research factor to consider is that the municipal codes are usually published in looseleaf format. This has an impact on the research process because looseleaf services are updated by removing the outdated page and inserting the current page. Before an ordinance can be cited, it is important to confirm that the page that is in the binder is the most current page. To do this, the publisher generally has a designation at the bottom of the page which identifies the issuance of the material by date or number. This information must be compared with pages in the front of the binder which are generally called "checklists."

Updating a municipal code presents another problem. The frequency of updating the code will vary. Thus, new information may be supplied on a frequent or irregular basis. For specific information on this point, contact the city or county clerk.

Municipal codes have one major distinguishing characteristic: they are rarely annotated. This has a significant impact on the research method for finding interpretive case law. Because there are no cases readily available, alternative sources must be consulted. The most common source is *SHEPARD'S* state citators. In the statute edition, there is a section designated for the municipal codes; the interpretive case law can be found by looking under the city's name and the subject matter of the ordinance.

Although not as efficient as finding the provision in *SHEPARD'S*, it is possible to locate interpretive cases by three other methods. The first source is the *state digest*. By analyzing the facts to find a case in the digest as discussed in Chapter 1, the researcher can find the appropriate topic and key number. The second source is a *treatise*. There are two major treatises in the area of municipal law which are updated on a regular basis. They are E. McQuillin, *Law of Municipal Corporations* and C. Antieau, *Municipal Corporation Law*. Although these sources are available, the researcher should be aware that they are not the most efficient method of finding interpretive case law. The third source is *Ordinance Law Annotations*, published by West and updated annually. These volumes organize the material according to subject matter and list the relevant cases. The set also has a two-volume table of cases organized by state and county or city.

LOOKING FOR A CITY ORDINANCE?

Are you looking for an answer to a local problem? If so, check:

___ 1.   The city charter if it is like a constitutional issue; or,

___ 2.   The city ordinance if it is more like a statutory problem.

If a local problem exists, how do you find the local charter or ordinance?

___ 3.   Use the topic method if you are familiar with the code;

___ 4.   Use the descriptive word method in the code's general index section if you are not familiar with the organization of the material; or,

___ 5.   Use secondary sources such as a treatise if you need a general description of local law.

If you need to do a comparative study of municipal ordinances, how do you get the information?

___ 6.   Use *Ordinance Law Annotations;* or,

___ 7.   Use secondary sources such as one of the two major treatises on municipal corporations.

This problem is based on the San Antonio, Texas, City Code. The research process will be similar for other city codes.

EXAMPLE: Your client's dog, Prosser, is a large, loud animal who likes to bark. In fact, the next door neighbor has complained on several occasions that Prosser barks all day long when he is left outside while your client is at work. The neighbor wants your client to do something about this problem because he has a night job and needs to sleep during the day, which is impossible to do because of Prosser's constant barking. Your client does nothing to restrain Prosser. The

issue is whether your client has violated any city laws by
allowing the dog to bark.

[3] Finding and Updating a City Ordinance

As with other legislative problems, the first step is to analyze the facts
according to the TAPP rule. The key word in this situation is "noise." The
following process should be used:

1. *Index:* Use the key words and phrases in the Index to the
    City Code. A caveat: the Code may have two indices — one
    for the city charter and the other for the ordinances. Be
    certain that you are in the proper index or else you will not
    find the information. In this case, the index for the ordi-
    nances is in the back of the Code. Under the term "noise,"
    the definitions appear in § 21-52.

2. *Read and Analyze the Provision:* The researcher must read
    the relevant section. § 21-52(a)(3) prohibits the keeping of
    an animal which makes frequent or long continuous noise,
    so the client has violated the Code.

3. *Update the Provision:* The researcher must note the page
    number where the provision is found and the date or
    supplement number at the bottom of the page. This infor-
    mation is important in the updating process.

    The next step is to turn to the checklist in the front of the
    volume to ensure that the most recent information is in the
    binder. Sometimes there will be discrepancies in these
    numbers. However, if the number at the bottom of the page
    of the text is at least as large as the number on the
    checklist, then the information is current. In the present
    case, the information is up-to-date.

4. *Shepardize the Provision:* The researcher must verify and
    update the information. This can be accomplished through
    SHEPARD'S. The researcher would need to Shepardize this
    provision in *SHEPARD'S Texas Citations,* statutes vol-
    umes, under the ordinance section, which is arranged by
    cities' names and the subject matter of the ordinance.
    SHEPARD'S will indicate whether the provision has been
    held constitutional or valid by a court.

[4] Finding and Updating Interpretive Cases

The next step in the research process is to find interpretive case law.
This may be done in several ways. The most common methods are outlined
below:

1. *Annotated Codes:* Sometimes a municipal code will be
    annotated, but this is rare.

2. *Shepardize: SHEPARD'S Texas Citations*, statutes volumes, in the ordinance section will list the code topic and any interpretive case citations.

3. *Secondary Authority:* Secondary resources such as the following will provide case authority:

   a. *Ordinance Law Annotations*;

   b. Treatises such as:

   (1) E. McQuillin, *Law of Municipal Corporations*; or,

   (2) C. Antieau, *Municipal Corporations Law*.

MUNICIPAL CODE CHECKLIST

1. Analyze the facts according to the TAPP rule.
2. Use the key words and phrases in the code index. Caveat: be sure it is the index for ordinances and not for the city charter.
3. Read the relevant section.
4. Note the page number and the supplement number or date at the bottom of the page.
5. Use the checklist sheets, usually located at the front of the volume, to determine whether the information is current.
6. Find interpretive case law by:
   a. *SHEPARD'S Texas Citations*, statutes volumes, under ordinance section for the city's name and the subject of the ordinance;
   b. state digest to access through the usual case search process;
   c. secondary sources such as a treatise; or,
   d. *Ordinance Law Annotations*.
7. Verify both the provision and cases by using the appropriate state volumes of *SHEPARD'S*.

Computer Note

LEXIS-NEXIS and WESTLAW provide access to a few city codes and charters. **Internet** availability is expanding rapidly. **Internet** access to city charters and codes in over forty states is available at the Municipal Laws Corporation website: <http://www.municode.com/database.html>.

Chapter 7

STATE ADMINISTRATIVE RESEARCH

§ A ADMINISTRATIVE LAW ORGANIZATION

The administrative function of the states is similar to that at the federal level. State agencies exercise power delegated to them through the governor or the state legislature. As government grows more complex at all levels, states require expanded administrative organization. The legal researcher should be aware of the daily importance of state administrative operations and be ready to locate any materials relevant to legal problems at the state level.

[1] Official Sources

State administrative materials, like their federal counterparts, take many forms. The governor's office issues orders and directives that will affect the operation of state agencies. State agencies issue licenses, orders, decisions, and rules interpreting and enforcing state statutes. Once again, these rules generally have the greatest impact of all administrative functions, and the alert researcher will be sure to check for the existence of such provisions. These provisions, however, do not exist in a vacuum and, like federal rules and regulations, are subject to interpretation by state and even federal courts. All research into state rules, then, will include the extra steps of finding any interpretive cases.

This process is complicated by the fact that publication of state administrative materials is chaotic at best and nonexistent at worst. In addition, there is no consistent pattern of publication from state to state. A few general statements, however, can be made about official publication of state rules and regulations. They generally appear first in a state "register" similar to the *Federal Register.* They may be issued on a weekly, bi-weekly, or monthly basis, and some have no indexing system. The *Texas Register,* for example, is published twice weekly and includes proposed rules and regulations, items from the Governor, changes in or repeals of existing state rules, as well as a summary of state statutes enacted. The *Texas Register* includes annual and quarterly indices, with monthly updates available at the Secretary of State's website.

Over forty states now have official administrative codes which are arranged by subject matter. For example, the *Texas Administrative Code* (*T.A.C.*) is published by West in sixteen titles with fifty ultimately projected. Each title is divided into parts, chapters, subchapters and sections. Every title contains rules still in force, incorporating new provisions and deleting those revoked. Updating patterns for the codes will vary from state to state.

[2] Unofficial Sources

State administrative materials are generally published by the state or by official state sanction. There are some unofficial sources, however, that provide explanations of these materials. Probably the best source for determining how each state's administrative documents are published and updated is M. L. Fisher's *Guide to State Legislative and Administrative Materials,* 4th ed. This volume identifies the sources available and their update procedures, and includes addresses of the Secretary of State and other pertinent officials. Another source of state agencies, functions and officers is *The Book of the States* biennially published by the Council of State Governments. The most useful tool, however, for descriptions of state agencies is a manual produced by most state governments which is similar to the *U.S. Government Manual.* The *Texas State Directory,* for example, appears annually and includes addresses and phone numbers for all branches of state and local government. This is the best source to use when information is needed about a particular agency or its rules. In addition, many state agencies now have their own websites.

§ B STATE RULE AND REGULATION LOCATION METHODS

The methods of finding state rules and regulations depend upon the organization of each state's administrative code. For the purposes of this discussion, the *T.A.C.* is used as the model.

LOOKING FOR A STATE RULE OR REGULATION?

Use one of the following methods:

___ 1. Descriptive Word Method; or,

___ 2. Topic Method.

EXAMPLE: A vehicle owner in Texas wants a license plate for his car to include his initials and the abbreviation "J.D." He wants to know whether any state regulation governs the contents of vanity plates.

[1] Descriptive Word Method

This is the most likely means of locating a state rule. Using the basic descriptive word method that emphasizes the TAPP rule, go to the paperbound *Texas Administrative Code* General Index.

Things:	automobile, vehicle
Acts:	application for vanity plate
Persons:	vehicle owner
Places:	license plate

Because the titles and chapter names are broad, the words "vehicle" and "license plates" appear to be the best prospects for such an index. The word "vehicle" cross references to "motor vehicles," and "license plates" is classified as "license number plates." Both phrases direct the researcher to "motor vehicles," where a subcategory under "license number plates" directs specifically to "personalized license plates" at "Transportation—Title 43" in Chapter 17, Section 28. Within that section are the rules governing the issuance of personalized license plates.

[2] Topic Method

If the researcher has some familiarity with the titles in the state code, she may proceed directly to the relevant title and consult the individual subject index at the end of the title. Using this method, the researcher would go directly to Title 43 and turn to the subject index where the research process would continue in the manner applicable to the descriptive word method. Once the state rule is located, it should be read carefully. Source notes follow the provision and explain the history of the rule, *i.e.*, when the rule was adopted or changed. Citations of Authority provide statutory or other authority for the rule, similar to enabling legislation at the federal level.

§ C   UPDATING A STATE RULE

To update state rules, follow the procedures listed below:

1. *Certification Date:* Check the effectiveness date at the front of the volume or the front of any supplementary pamphlet.

2. *Texas Register Index:* Depending upon the effectiveness date, check the quarterly and/or weekly *Texas Administrative Code Titles Affected* list arranged by title and section number. The quarterly list appears in the quarterly index to the *Texas Register* and the weekly list is available at the Secretary of State's home page.

3. *Bi-Weekly Texas Register:* Check the individual issues published twice weekly.

4. *Shepardize:* State rules CANNOT be Shepardized.

§ D   FINDING AND UPDATING INTERPRETIVE CASES

Interpretive cases can be located in the following manner:

1. *Digest:* Use the basic descriptive word method in the *Texas Digest* to locate interpretive cases because the *T.A.C.* provides no Notes of Decision.

2. *Regional Reporter:* Go to the appropriate reporter and read the case.

3. *Agency Decisions*: Available officially from the agency on a sporadic basis, sometimes accessible through an agency website.

4. *SHEPARD'S:* Shepardize the case in the appropriate *SHEP-ARD'S* volumes.

Computer Note

LEXIS-NEXIS and **WESTLAW** provide coverage of a number of state administrative codes, such as the *T.A.C.*, as well as state registers, including the *Texas Register*. **Internet** access may be available at a Secretary of State's website.

STATE RULES AND REGULATIONS CHECKLIST

1. Analyze the fact situation according to the TAPP rule.
2. Locate the relevant rule or regulation by:
   a. the General Subject Method; or,
   b. the Agency Name Method in the paperbound *T.A.C.* General Index issued annually.
3. Read the provision and check the Source Notes and Citations of Authority.
4. Update the rule or regulation by:
   a. Effectiveness Date;
   b. *Texas Register Index — T.A.C. Titles Affected*, issued quarterly and weekly (also available at Secretary of State's website); and,
   c. *Texas Register* individual issues — issued twice weekly.
5. Find and update interpretive cases by:
   a. the Descriptive Word Method in the *Texas Digest*;
   b. reporter volume: read the case in the appropriate reporter;
   c. or agency decisions issued sporadically by the state agency available through the agency; and,
   d. Sheparardizing any relevant judicial decisions in the appropriate *SHEPARD'S* volumes.

Chapter 8

SECONDARY SOURCE RESEARCH

§ A SECONDARY SOURCE ORGANIZATION

Most of this guide has been dedicated to finding primary authority because that is the goal of the researcher. However, secondary authority can play a valid role in the research process. Furthermore, there is a hierarchy of secondary authority which will be discussed in this chapter.

Secondary authority is not the law itself; it is an analysis or explanation of primary authority. Although secondary authority should be cited infrequently in a legal memorandum or appellate brief, it can serve an important purpose in the research process.

There are two functions of secondary authority. The first is as a means of finding primary authority. As a research tool, the most valuable parts of these sources are the references, because they provide the researcher with primary authority such as cases, statutes, or administrative codes, rules, and regulations. The second function of secondary authority is to provide insight into and background information on a particular problem. Thus, secondary authority can provide an overview of a subject or basic understanding to an area of law with which the researcher is unfamiliar.

Before using secondary authority, the researcher should ask certain questions about the advisability of using this type of source. The following checklist provides some guidance as to its value and the response to the researcher's mental query.

CHECKLIST FOR USING SECONDARY AUTHORITY

1. Is there any primary authority from the jurisdiction where the case is being litigated?

   a. If this is a "case of first impression," then the court will be more receptive to reviewing the secondary authority.

   b. If the case presents a novel issue, then a source that weighs the merits of the issue is helpful.

2. Is secondary authority being used as a substitute for primary authority?

   a. If yes, then do not use it.

   b. If no, then it may be used to bolster the legal argument.

3. Is the secondary authority merely repetitive of the primary sources that are being used?

   a. If yes, then delete the reference to it.

   b. If no, then use it sparingly.

4. Will the source aid the court in its interpretation of primary authority?

   a. If yes, then it may be used, particularly if it is a new area of law or one where there has not been much litigation.

   b. If no, then it is irrelevant.

5. Is emphasis and a place of prominence given to secondary authority in the legal memorandum or appellate brief?

   a. If yes, then reassess its use because too great an emphasis is being given to it.

   b. If no, then use it wisely and sparingly.

6. Is there a proper foundation or predicate for the secondary source? Corollary issues to this point include the following questions:

   a. Is the source reliable?

      (1) The quality of the product depends on the reputation and skill of the author.

      (2) It also depends on the reputation of the publisher, *i.e.*, for accuracy, etc.

   b. Is there contradictory primary authority?

      (1) Court opinions, statutes, or the constitution will control.

7. If the secondary source is critical of a recent decision which has charted a new line of reasoning or has incorrectly applied the law, then there may be a valid role for the commentary.

§ B HIERARCHY OF SECONDARY AUTHORITY

All secondary authority is *not* created equal! There are differences in these sources both in the weight of their authority and the likelihood of finding pertinent information. However, a typical reaction of a novice researcher is to use the first source without analyzing why that source is appropriate or inappropriate. It is the goal of this chapter to provide some insight on the use of secondary authority and why certain sources are more effective than others. Therefore, the discussion of secondary authority will consist of a brief description of that source; an itemization of the purposes of the particular material; some suggestions for appropriate ways to use the source within this hierarchy of secondary authority; and finally, a checklist describing the process of research for each source.

[1] Attorney General Opinions

[a] Description

Attorney General Opinions exist at both the federal and state levels of government. The Attorney General is the counsel for the government. Consequently, government officials can make a written request for her legal opinion on particular governmental matters. Three preliminary requirements must be met: (1) there must be an actual problem; (2) the problem must be presented to the Attorney General before the state or federal government is involved in civil or criminal litigation; and, (3) it must be a question of law and not fact.

The Attorney General's opinions combine aspects of both primary and secondary authority. They are primary in the sense that they are opinions which are written like a judicial opinion and are supported by primary authority, and therefore, they are very persuasive. For example, there is a Supreme Court case where an auditor abused his discretion because he refused to follow an Attorney General Opinion. The opinions are also secondary in nature because they are only advisory opinions and are not binding or mandatory. Because of this dual status, Attorney General Opinions can be placed at the top of the secondary authority hierarchy.

[b] Purpose

Attorney General Opinions fulfill two purposes. First, through these opinions the Attorney General gives legal advice to the President or Governor, as the case may be, or to the legislature and administrative agencies. Second, she construes statutes and interprets judicial decisions and administrative regulations, particularly where the effect of the primary authority is uncertain.

[c] Use

When a researcher has a legislative problem, some consideration should be given to checking for an Attorney General Opinion. Opinions are an effective source of authority because: (1) they are written in response to specific inquiries by a government official about a current problem and not just an abstract or moot issue; (2) they are written in the style of a judicial opinion and supported with primary authority instead of being merely the "opinion" of the Attorney General; and, (3) they are noted as cited references in *SHEPARD'S United States Citations, U.S. Administrative Citations, Federal Citations,* and state citators.

[d] Location Method

EXAMPLE: On September 5, 1984, the Travis County Attorney requested that the Attorney General of Texas construe article 6675a-9a, V.T.C.S. so that the county would know when it could impose an optional county vehicle registration fee on license plate renewals. The ambiguous language arose over two provisions of the act. One section indicated that the fee was effective "beginning January 1 of a year ending in a '5' or a '0'." Another provision from the same act stated that the fee applies to "a registration period that begins on or after the date the fee takes effect."

On December 28, 1984, the Attorney General responded to the Travis County Attorney. His opinion included cites to the act, legislative history, and case authority. It also included relevant secondary authority concerning the definition of the word "month." Specifically, definitions were obtained from *Texas Jurisprudence*, a local encyclopedia, and a dictionary.

Computer Note

Both **LEXIS-NEXIS** and **WESTLAW** have databases for Attorney General Opinions. **WESTLAW** has all 50 states and **LEXIS-NEXIS** has 48 states except for Nebraska and Vermont. In most states, the database extends back to 1977. In recent years, opinions from the United States Attorney General have been issued rarely. **LEXIS-NEXIS'** GENFED Library, USAG file has these Attorney General Opinions since 1791. **WESTLAW** also has a USAG database with opinions dating back to 1791. Attorney General Opinions may also be found on the **Internet**. For example, Attorney General Opinions are available for all 50 states, the District of Columbia, American Samoa, Guam, Puerto Rico, and the Virgin Islands at <http://www.naag.org/aglinks.htm>.

CHECKLIST FOR ATTORNEY GENERAL OPINIONS

1. To locate an Attorney General Opinion:
   a. check the individual index for the annual bound volume of opinions;
   b. check the digest of opinions if available;
   c. Shepardize any relevant case or statute to determine if an Attorney General Opinion is a cited reference; and,
   d. check secondary sources to find an opinion cited in a footnote.
2. Read the relevant opinion in the bound volume:
   a. The opinions are reported in their full text in annual bound volumes.
   b. They are also available on microfilm.
3. Update the Attorney General Opinions:
   a. There is no formal updating process. The index and digest are the best ways to determine if additional opinions have been issued on a topic.
   b. As a general rule, opinions cannot be Shepardized.

---

[2] *Restatements*

[a] Description

The *Restatements* of the law were begun in 1923 by the American Law Institute to simplify the case law by providing a clear and systematic restatement of it. It was the hope of the drafters of the *Restatement, First Series*, that the volumes would serve as a substitute for the codification of the law. However, this hope never became a reality.

Restatements provide the reader with a "black letter" statement of the law, an explanatory comment, examples of the principles, and variations of them. *Restatement, Second Series*, states new trends in the common law and will advocate what the rule will be or should be. In addition, the *Restatements* can be a good research tool. They provide case authority for the statements and cross references to West's topics and key numbers, as well as *A.L.R.* annotations.

Moreover, the *Restatements* have had an impact on the courts. Of all the types of commentaries, the *Restatements* are the most respected. This is evident by several series that are published for the purpose of citing cases that have applied or interpreted the *Restatements*. For example, West published a series called *Restatement in the Courts* until 1977. A few of the *Restatements* have been updated since that time. Since 1976, *SHEPARD'S* has published a separate citator for the *Restatements*. In addition, separate volumes with annotations of court decisions have been provided in many states. For example, there are California annotations to the *Restatement of the Law of Torts*.

[b] Purpose

The *Restatements* fulfill several purposes. First, they provide an orderly statement of the common law. Second, they promote the classification and simplification of the law. Third, they provide suggestions for the law's adaptation to social needs and the better administration of justice. And finally, they provide a thorough review of the subject with cases on both sides of the issue as well as the drafters' commentary and illustrations.

[c] Use

Whether a *Restatement* is used in a research problem will be determined by the subject matter of the issue and the particular need that counsel has in the case. Concerning subject matter, the case must involve one of the ten topics that are included in the *Restatements*. This means that the researcher will be limited to the areas of agency, conflict of laws, contracts, foreign relations law, judgments, property, restitution, security, torts, and trusts. An additional limitation is that they are not mandatory or binding on the court because they lack legislative sanction. Concerning the needs of counsel, one might use the *Restatements* to: (1) support an argument that advocates either social change or an improvement to the justice system; (2) support an argument by experts within a particular field; or (3) support an argument where the court is faced with a case of first impression.

The effectiveness of the *Restatements* has varied from field to field. However, overall they have been very successful and have had considerable influence on the court. The publication itself has been accepted largely because of the intellectual scrutiny that has been given to each section of the *Restatements*. This acceptance primarily has been due to the scholarship of the authors and the publication. For instance, the authors include either well known scholars in the field or outstanding members of the judiciary.

[d] Location Methods

EXAMPLE: Briner brought a cause of action against Hyslop for injuries sustained as a result of the negligent conduct of the corporation's employee. The issue was whether the corporation should be liable for punitive damages if it could have prevented the wrongful conduct of its employee.

This is a case of first impression in Iowa. Therefore, counsel needs to present persuasive authority that the corporation should not only be liable for the hiring and training of its employees, but it should also be held responsible where it could have prevented the employee's wrongful conduct.

It would be appropriate for counsel to search the *Restatement of Torts* for a solution to this case of first impression. In an actual case, the Iowa Supreme Court adopted the *Restatement* view.

Computer Note

Both **LEXIS-NEXIS** and **WESTLAW** have added a *Restatement* file. On **LEXIS-NEXIS**, the researcher can begin in Library, Restat file. On **WESTLAW**, it is the REST database. In addition, it is possible to use a particular section number as a key word in an inquiry to retrieve cases that have cited the *Restatement*.

CHECKLIST FOR THE *RESTATEMENTS*

1. Find the *Restatement* provision by using:
   a. The General Index for the first series;
   b. The Individual Index for both series by individual subjects;
   c. The Topic Method by checking the Table of Contents for each *Restatement*; and,
   d. Other secondary sources by checking for periodicals in the appropriate indices.
2. Read the relevant provision in the bound volumes.
3. Review the aids that are available such as the explanatory comments, illustrations, court citations, and cross references.
4. If the *Restatements* are used as a research tool for case authority, be sure to read the cases themselves and Shepardize them in the appropriate citator.
5. Update the information:
   a. *First Series*: See the appendices in the *Second Series*.
   b. Prior to 1977: See *Restatement in the Courts*.
   c. Since 1976: See the pocket parts in the *Second Series*.
6. Shepardize the provision in *SHEPARD'S Restatement of the Law Citations*.

---

[3] Law Review Articles

[a] Description

Law reviews are produced by major American law schools and have been in existence since the mid-1800s. Articles are divided into three categories depending on the author. For example, lead articles are written by scholars and practitioners who do an extensive analysis of a subject. Notes and Comments are written by law students. "Comments" are generally longer and provide more depth than a student case "Note."

[b] Purpose

Law review articles fulfill several purposes. First, they provide a serious analysis of current legal issues, particularly judicial opinions. There is also some coverage of statutory provisions and administrative regulations. Second, they provide historical research. Articles will generally trace the history of the case law in that particular area of law. Third, articles may incorporate empirical studies or interdisciplinary aspects of legal problems. Fourth, they help to formulate legal policy arguments. Finally, they provide a research tool for cites to both primary and secondary sources. Typically, law review articles are rich in footnotes that cite to both primary and secondary authority.

[c] Use

Law review articles are helpful if the research involves case authority, particularly if the research focuses on a new area of law, if a recent or controversial case is relevant, or if inter-disciplinary research is needed. Law review articles have proven an effective source of authority because: (1) the editorial board exercises control over the acceptance of the articles, which ensures serious scholarship; and, (2) they provide the most thorough discussion of new legal developments and issues.

[d] Location Method

EXAMPLE: John Miles worked at a nuclear power plant for five years. During that time, he was exposed to radiation and subsequently died. His widow seeks your advice on the liability of the plant operators and the damages she can obtain for his death.

There are two ways to locate a law review article. One method focuses on the general subject matter; in this instance, the general subject matter is liability for nuclear accidents which is an emerging area of the law. The second method of finding a law review article involves research through case names such as *Silkwood v. Kerr-McGee Corporation*, which is the leading case in the area. Using the Index's Table of Cases, this case could lead to numerous law review articles.

Computer Note

Both **LEXIS-NEXIS** and **WESTLAW** have added a legal periodical database. Although it is not comprehensive, there is a constantly growing number of law journals and A.B.A. publications that are being added to the databases. Through **LEXIS-NEXIS'** LAWREV library and **WESTLAW**'s TP database (text and periodicals), the text and footnotes of these articles can be retrieved. On the **Internet**, the researcher might try the electronic equivalent to the *Index to Legal Periodicals and Books* which indexes more than 750 English-language legal periodicals. That site is <http://wilsonweb3.hwwilson.com/cgi-bin/auto_login.cgi>. Legaltrac is the electronic equivalent of the *Current Law Index* and indexes approximately 900 English-language legal periodicals. That site is <http://infotrac.galegroup.com/twel>.

CHECKLIST FOR LAW REVIEW ARTICLES

1. Find the law review article by:

   a. the *Index to Legal Periodicals* (*I.L.P.*) through its listing by:

      (1) subject/author;

      (2) table of cases commented upon;

      (3) table of statutes commented upon; or,

      (4) book reviews.

   b. the *Current Law Index* (*C.L.I.*) began in 1980 and indexes more periodicals than the *I.L.P.* Access to the article cites is the same as the *I.L.P.*:

      (1) subject index;

      (2) author/title index;

      (3) table of cases commented upon;

      (4) table of statutes commented upon; or,

      (5) book reviews.

2. Read the article, carefully examining:

   a. the text for policy arguments, historical information, and analysis; and,

   b. the footnotes for references to other primary and secondary authority.

3. Read, analyze, and update the information that is found in the text and footnotes.

4. *SHEPARD'S Law Review Citations* provides a means to update the information by listing courts and other law reviews that have cited the article.

[4] Treatises

[a] Description

Historically, treatises have been in existence since the fifteenth century. However, modern treatises are expositions on the case law and legislation. Treatises focus on a particular, narrow area of the law such as Blashfield on *Automobile Accidents* or Couch on *Insurance*. As a result, they are more comprehensive than some other forms of secondary authority such as an encyclopedia.

In addition, the term "treatise" refers to different forms of commentary. There are both *single* volume and *multi-volume* sets; there are *hornbooks*, which are student texts that introduce the terms and concepts of a particular legal field; *monographs*, which are one volume in length, narrow in scope, and are rarely supplemented; *practice guides*, which are designed for the practitioner in a particular area of law; and *handbooks for laymen*, which are very general in nature and include simplified instructions for conducting legal business.

Although the forms may vary, there are certain common characteristics to most treatises. For instance, treatises are written in narrative style with a general discussion of the point. This information is supported by footnotes with references to both primary and secondary authority. Charts and appendices are also common in treatises. All of these materials can be located through an index at the back of the volume.

[b] Purpose

Treatises will: (1) summarize the historical developments in that particular field of law; (2) analyze and explain any inconsistencies in the law; (3) predict future changes to the law; and, (4) provide practical insights into courtroom procedure and methods of conducting business.

[c] Use

Treatises can be a valuable research tool. For example, a treatise gives the researcher the perspective of the author on a particular subject; it provides interpretation of statutes and case law; it is a means of finding cases; and it presents the general principles, exceptions, and variations in an area of law.

The disadvantage is that the quality of the treatise depends on the author and his reputation, knowledge, and skill. The quality will also depend on the publisher and the accuracy of cites and text.

[d] Location Method

EXAMPLE: The issue to be resolved is whether a parody falls within parameters of the "fair use" doctrine under the copyright law.

Due to the nature of the problem, it may be advisable for the researcher to begin with a treatise if the researcher is unfamiliar with the general terms of copyright law. The following checklist will demonstrate the research procedure.

CHECKLIST FOR A TREATISE

1. Find a treatise by:
    a. the card catalog at the law library under title, subject, or author's name; or,
    b. recommendation of others.

2. Evaluate the quality of the treatise by:
    a. the reputation and stature of the author;
    b. the reputation of the publisher;
    c. the purpose and originality of the work;
    d. the research aids that are available; and,
    e. the frequency of the supplementation.

3. Find the relevant section in the treatise by:
    a. the subject index at the back of the book or possibly in separate volumes if the treatise is a multi-volume set;
    b. the table of contents in the beginning of the book; or,
    c. the table of cases or statutes if you already have one good case or statute.

4. Read the section.

5. Review the footnotes for cases and other relevant information.

6. Update the information. Generally this is through an annual pocket part. However, be sure to check the date on the pocket part to see how recent it is so that the material can be updated from that point through other conventional updating procedures.

7. Read the relevant cases or statutes from the text of that material.

8. Update all relevant information in the appropriate volumes of *SHEPARD'S* citators.

Computer Note

At the present time, there are a few treatises on **WESTLAW** in the text and periodicals (TP) database. **LEXIS-NEXIS** has the *Blue Sky Reporter*, some local encyclopedias such as *Tex. Jur. 3d*, *Fla. Jur. 2d*, *N.Y. Jur. 2d*, and *Ohio Jur. 3d*, and some California materials such as Witkin's *Summary of California Law*, Witkin & Epstein's *Criminal Law* (2d ed.), Witkin's *California Procedure* (3d ed.), and Witkin's *California Evidence* (3d ed.). On the **Internet**, there is a subscription website called Indexmaster which has the indexes and tables of contents of over 4000 legal treatises on a wide variety of subjects. For best access, the researcher should use Netscape browser. Access through <http://www.indexmaster.com>.

---

[5] Legal Encyclopedias

[a] Description

Legal encyclopedias, while valuable as a reference, have little weight in persuading a court to accept a particular position. There are several reasons for this view. Generally speaking, legal encyclopedias place emphasis on case authority, but there is little treatment of statutory law. This factor alone is a great limitation on the resource and may present a distorted picture of the subject matter. In addition, the articles are not written by well-known scholars or jurists, and therefore, the reputation of the authors does not have the impact that a treatise by an expert in the field might have. Furthermore, in an effort to give a clear and concise statement of the law, encyclopedias tend to provide over-simplified and generalized treatment of the subject.

There are three types of legal encyclopedias. The first type is a *general* encyclopedia which discusses all American law. Examples of this type are *Corpus Juris Secondum (C.J.S.)* by West Group and *American Jurisprudence (Am. Jur.)*, formerly by Lawyers Cooperative Publishing, now by West Group. Although the format and research procedure for the two encyclopedias is virtually the same, there are major differences in the approach between the two publications. For example, *C.J.S.* purports to cover all cases, references are to its topic and key numbers, and there is limited statutory coverage. On the other hand, *Am. Jur.* uses only selected cases which it feels are the most important, it cites to its Total Client Service Library, which has more secondary sources, it has more statutory coverage, and it produces a Desk Book as a helpful quick reference to an array of information and data that might be needed by the practitioner.

The second type of encyclopedia is a *local* encyclopedia. These encyclopedias focus on a specific state. Fifteen states have encyclopedias. An example of a local encyclopedia is *Michie's Jurisprudence of Virginia and West Virginia*, published by LEXIS Publishing. The coverage and philosophy of these publications will differ depending on the publisher.

There are some advantages to the local encyclopedias over the general ones. For example, the researcher will find only the law of the jurisdiction that he is interested in and not law for all of the states. Furthermore, there tends to be greater coverage of statutory law in the local encyclopedias than in the general ones. At best, the general encyclopedia will state that a statute may apply or, as in *Am. Jur.*, the publisher will note selected statutes. Also, the local encyclopedias usually provide a table of statutes cited for ease in locating them in the text.

In addition to the local encyclopedias, the publishers may also produce state-specific supplementary materials for the practitioner which parallel their encyclopedias or digests. For example, West publishes an outline or summary of the law which is more limited than the encyclopedias such as *Summary of California Law* and *Summary of Mississippi Law*. West produces the state practice series, which are generally multi-volume sets but which are not as comprehensive as the encyclopedias. Examples of these include *California Practice, Massachusetts Practice Series, New Jersey Practice,* and *Louisiana Civil Law Treatise Series.* And finally, several publishers issue what are known as state law finders which try to consolidate access to both primary and secondary authority on a subject. Examples of this type of publication include *Illinois Law Finder, Massachusetts Law Finder, New York Law Finder, Pennsylvania Law Finder,* and *Texas Law Finder.*

The third type of encyclopedia is a special interest encyclopedia. West Group's Total Client Service Library produces what the company calls "how-to-do-it" books. For instance, *Am. Jur. Trials* is a special series that is an encyclopedic guide to modern trial practices, procedures, and strategies. It provides commentary by an expert in the field, cross references to other sources, checklists of questions to ask or things to do, sample forms or diagrams, and illustrations on how to compile evidence.

[b] Purpose

The purpose of these encyclopedias is twofold. First, they give a general discussion of the law. Depending on the type of encyclopedia, it will be a discussion of all American law or the law of a particular state. Second, they briefly summarize the rule of law and support the proposition with case authority and other cross references.

[c] Use

Legal encyclopedias are not an effective source to cite in a legal memorandum or an appellate brief. The court gives this form of secondary authority little weight because they are not scholarly writing and do not provide a detailed analysis or authoritative statement of the law.

In spite of these limitations, the legal encyclopedia can be a valuable research tool because it is a good starting point for legal research. If the researcher wants background information on an unfamiliar area of law, or wants a general overview of the subject, or needs a narrative introduction to basic concepts, then an encyclopedia is a good place to begin. In addition, the legal encyclopedia is a good tool for finding case authority for a proposition; however, the limitation of not having comprehensive legislative materials must be kept in mind. Encyclopedias also have definitions of important legal terms and legal maxims. Although it is not as comprehensive as a legal dictionary, the legal encyclopedia includes definitions of most important legal terms or legal maxims. Thus, if the research problem involves a definition, the encyclopedia might be one place to look.

[d] Location Method

EXAMPLE: Your clients, Joe and Ima Spectator, seek your advice concerning personal injuries they received while watching a baseball game when a foul ball struck them. Joe regularly attended games at the stadium and had season tickets for seats that were in the unscreened section behind first base. Ima was both uninterested in baseball and unknowledgeable of the possible dangers lurking in and about playing fields. The issue is whether the owners of the stadium are liable for the injuries sustained by Joe and Ima Spectator.

If a state were listed in the problem, then the researcher would start with a local encyclopedia such as *Texas Jurisprudence*. Because no state has been listed in this problem, use *Am. Jur. 2d*. This problem could be run through either a national or local encyclopedia. How the publisher catalogs the index may create differences in the key words and phrases that are used.

Due to the nature of the problem, this issue could be resolved through a case. Because the researcher is looking for a case, the fact analysis should follow that which was discussed under finding a case. The analysis might be as follows:

Parties:	spectators, patrons, owner, team, proprietor of sports arena
Places & Things:	baseball game, sports, amusement place, theatre, show, entertainment
Bases of Action:	negligence for failing to erect and maintain a screen, negligence for failing to warn of dangers, ignorance of potential dangers by the plaintiff
Defenses:	assumption of the risk, contributory negligence, duty of ordinary care
Relief Sought:	damages for negligence, medical expenses, court costs, attorney's fees

In the analysis, the key words or phrases for *Am. Jur. 2d* are "baseball" and "personal injuries." These key words and phrases would lead the researcher to 27A Am. Jur. 2d *Entertainment and Sports Law* § 80 (1996).

ENCYCLOPEDIA CHECKLIST

1. Analyze the facts according to Parties, Places, Basis of the Action, Defenses, and Relief Sought.

2. Use the key words and phrases in the General Index of the encyclopedia. Be sure to check any pocket part supplements to the General Index.

3. Turn to the appropriate title in the encyclopedia.

4. Scan both the Title Index and the Title Table of Contents for specific sections in order to obtain additional information and to understand the organization of the title.

5. Read the relevant provision for an understanding of the law.

6. For interpretive case law:

    a. check the Library References for digest topic and key number information if the encyclopedia is published by West; and,

    b. check the footnotes.

7. Update the information by using:

    a. the annual pocket part which will update both the text and the footnotes;

    b. the topic and key number in the relevant state digest which will provide more current information about recent cases; and,

    c. the topic and key number in the advance sheets of the relevant reporter which will also provide a case update for within the last six weeks.

8. Read, analyze, and Shepardize all of the relevant cases. It should be noted that West states that complete citation and full history are provided for each case. However, this is not a substitute for Shepardizing.

---

[6]   Legal Dictionaries

[a]   Description

The legal dictionary has been in existence since the sixteenth century. The first legal dictionary was written by John Rastell in England for the purpose of defining 208 obscure terms. Today, there are several types of legal dictionaries.

The first type of legal dictionary is categorized as a law dictionary. Two leading law dictionaries are *Black's Law Dictionary* and *Ballentine's Law Dictionary*. Typical features of these dictionaries include: a pronunciation guide; definitions of both modern and ancient terms; definitions of both English and foreign terms; cites to court decisions if the definition is from a case; and cross references to other sources. The type of cross references that are included depend upon the publisher. For example, *Black's Law Dictionary* has references to the *Restatements*, U.C.C., statutes, and court rules. *Ballentine's Law Dictionary* refers the reader to *A.L.R.* and *Am. Jur.* Concerning the number of terms, the dictionaries have grown from 208 obscure phrases to over 30,000 terms.

The second type of legal dictionary is a judicial dictionary. This type is exemplified by the series *Words and Phrases*. This set is published by West in ninety volumes and contains an alphabetical listing of the word or phrase followed by an abstract of the court decision that defined the word. These abstracts look like the case abstracts that are found in the digests. This publication is updated by annual pocket part supplements. A words and phrases section can also be found in various digests and the advance sheets of the reporters.

The third type of legal dictionary is a specialized dictionary. This type focuses on one particular area of law. For example, Kase has written a *Dictionary of Industrial Property and Related Terms.*

[b] Purpose

The legal dictionary has two basic functions. The first is to aid legal research by: clarifying the complexity of legal terminology; providing accurate and precise use of words and phrases; and clarifying the nuances, subtleties, and ambiguities of language. The second goal of a legal dictionary is to define legal terms, phrases, and concepts that would not be found in an ordinary dictionary.

[c] Use

Dictionaries are essentially tools for resolving a definitional problem; they are rarely used as cited authority. Thus, if the researcher has a definitional problem, there are three types of sources that could be consulted. Which source the researcher uses will depend on the type of term that is in question and the author of the source.

[d] Location Method

EXAMPLE: The statutory language of a Texas act is ambiguous about the term "month." The researcher needs to find a definition of that term to clarify the problem. How can the researcher find relevant information?

This problem can be resolved through using one of the definitional research aids that are available. The following checklist demonstrates the procedure that should be used.

DICTIONARY CHECKLIST

1. Determine which word or phrase is ambiguous.
2. Use one of the following sources:
   a. a law dictionary such as *Black's Law Dictionary* or *Ballentine's Law Dictionary*;
   b. a judicial dictionary such as *Words and Phrases*;
   c. a specialized dictionary if one exists for the topic. These could be located through the card catalog by checking the subject catalog;
   d. a local encyclopedia; or,
   e. possibly a general encyclopedia if the term could not be found in the local encyclopedia.
3. Update the information if possible:
   a. *Words and Phrases* can be updated through:
      (1) annual pocket part supplement;
      (2) those digests that have a words and phrases section; and,
      (3) the advance sheets of the reporter.
   b. encyclopedias can be updated through pocket parts.
4. If the term has been defined by a court, then look up the case and cite the definition from the court's opinion.
5. Shepardize any cases in the appropriate *SHEPARD'S* citator.

Computer Note

If the researcher does not understand a term while in a **WESTLAW** database, it is possible to type the word and use services menu under "di." This puts on the screen the relevant page in *Black's Law Dictionary*. To return to the original inquiry, the researcher simply uses the "Go Back" function key.

[7] Form Books

[a] Description

Many of the problems or transactions that occur in the practice of law are similar. This fact has led to the development of legal forms. Since the eighteenth century, lawyers have been able to purchase single printed forms at a legal stationers. As time went on, individual practitioners and law firms retained forms they had used in their practice so that they could be modified and reused in similar future transactions. Today, standard form books have become a major part of legal literature.

There are five types of form books. The first type is a general encyclopedic kind with extensive indices, annotations to cases, references to statutes and other primary sources, tax notes, cross references to other relevant materials, and regular pocket part supplementation. Examples of this multi-volume, encyclopedic type of a form book are West's *Modern Legal Forms*, *Am. Jur. Legal Forms*, and *Am. Jur. Pleading and Practice Forms*.

In addition to these major works, the second type of form book is a specialized form book which specializes in a particular subject of law. These form books are commonly found in areas such as real estate transactions, wills, and corporate practice.

The third type of form book may be part of the state practice guides as discussed under encyclopedias. The state practice guide forms are coordinated with the text material in the guide so that the practitioner has a handy reference to the text, acts, court rules, and forms. Two examples of this type of form book are *Douglas Forms* (North Carolina) and *Virginia Forms*, both of which are published by LEXIS Publishing.

The fourth type of form book is a statutory form book. The forms in these books are coordinated with the state codes. References are made to the code provision and its annotations. Their function is to meet the specific statutory requirements that are outlined in the code section.

The final type of form "book" has come into existence with the development of computer technology. Computer-assisted drafting, as it is called, is a means of storing and retrieving complete legal documents and forms. The American Bar Association has conducted studies and experiments about the feasibility of this type of word processing. In addition, numerous commercial firms such as Matthew Bender and Michie (both part of LEXIS Publishing) have software programs to provide this type of information.

[b] Purpose

The purpose of form books is three-fold. First, they provide standard forms that can be used and re-used by practitioners. These forms can be divided into two categories: (1) forms of instrument, *i.e.*, forms that effectuate legal transactions such as contracts, wills, or leases; and (2) forms of practice, *i.e.*, forms that are part of the business before the courts or administrative agencies such as various motions, pleadings, or judgments. The second purpose of form books is to provide a practical dimension to the law. In other words, it is the "how-to-do-it" aspect of law practice. Finally, form books provide summaries of the law and checklists that give meaning and substance to the form.

[c] Use

There is no argument that the use of form books is an important aid to office practice and that they are commonly used by practitioners. However, the researcher must keep in mind the advantages and disadvantages to using a form.

There are several advantages to using form books. First, they save tremendous time and effort. If a form has already been prepared, it saves the researcher's time in preparing a new document. The second advantage is a corollary of the first. The researcher has the benefit of using a standard document which incorporates the expertise of others, legal precedents, and statutory requirements. In other words, the researcher is not left alone to create the "perfect" document.

The third advantage of form books is that they are annotated, have notes on the tax consequences of a provision, and are keyed to applicable statutes. These research aids provide the assurance that the forms are correct and have been approved by the courts, legislature, or bar association. A final benefit is that they are frequently supplemented so that changes in the law are reflected in the forms.

In spite of these advantages, there are two disadvantages. These disadvantages are associated with the care that the researcher must use in copying a form. The first caveat is that wholesale copying of the form is dangerous. The form must be carefully and thoroughly read. Provisions that would be inappropriate or detrimental to the client must be removed and other language added. The second caveat is that modifications must be made for the specific facts and circumstances of each transaction. It would be a violation of professional responsibility for the researcher to disregard these caveats.

[d]   Location Methods

EXAMPLE: A client comes to your office because he wants to purchase a condominium. He asks you to write a deed for the condominium. Where would you look to find such a form?

A sample deed could be found in a form book. The following checklist will demonstrate the research steps in locating such an instrument:

FORM BOOK CHECKLIST

1. Find the relevant section in a form book by:

   a. Topic Method: Use the Topic Method if you know the general topic area where the form is likely to appear. Once in the appropriate volume and chapter, use the detailed outline at the beginning of the chapter to obtain the proper form.

   b. Descriptive Word Method: If you do not know where it might be located, then analyze your facts according to the TAPP rule and use those key words and phrases in the General Index. This analysis will provide the proper chapter and section number.

2. Read the introductory materials, checklists, and other research guides to become familiar with the law, requirements, and any caveats that the author may suggest.

3. Read carefully and thoroughly the appropriate form. Do not use a wholesale copy of the form.

4. Make appropriate changes in paragraphs or words to tailor the form to your client's needs.

5. Update the information by checking the pocket parts. The supplement will give up-to-date information on new forms, tax notes, how to use the forms, and other relevant information.

---

[8] Legal Directories

[a] Description

There are various types of directories. Some directories compile a national list of attorney data, while others are specialized directories for specific fields of law, jurisdictional directories for state or regional areas, or judicial directories which list the national or regional information about judges. However, the most pertinent directory for the purposes of this book is Martindale-Hubbell Law Directory, and therefore, it will be the focus of this section.

[b] Purpose

Martindale-Hubbell serves two purposes. The first is to provide a listing of attorneys who have been admitted to the bar of any jurisdiction. This multi-volume set is published annually and lists attorneys alphabetically by state and city, by bar roster, and by law firms. In addition, the directory has a rating system whereby an attorney can be rated according to legal ability, ethical standards, professional reliability, and other such criteria. Attorneys may request not to have a rating.

The last volume of Martindale-Hubbell is the law digest volume of uniform acts. This volume is a comprehensive digest of laws from the states, federal government, and territories. It is compiled under approximately 100 major subject headings and up to 500 subheadings which the editors feel are the most useful to the legal profession. It also has notations about the forms of instrument that are used by that state or jurisdiction.

[c] Use

The initial volumes that comprise the directory are a helpful aid in locating attorneys. They also help law students to learn something about the law firms and attorneys before they begin job interviews.

The law digest volume is a quick resource for determining the particular uniform laws of the states. It provides information about the uniform laws as well as the statutory provisions of the states and some foreign countries through abstracts. Although it is a helpful reference, the researcher should not rely on these abstracts as official or definitive information. As with case abstracts in the digest or other resources, the information should always be confirmed in the original text such as the code or reporter.

[d] Location Method

EXAMPLE: Your client made a will in Florida but died while residing in Texas. To administer his estate, you need to know if Texas has the Uniform Probate of Foreign Wills Act. Without checking the Texas Code provisions, how could you answer this question?

This problem could be resolved by using the Martindale-Hubbell Law Directory. The following checklist demonstrates the procedure:

MARTINDALE-HUBBELL CHECKLIST

1. Locate the last volume of Martindale-Hubbell which is the law digest volume.

2. Find the section for Texas.

3. Look under the appropriate subject headings. In this case, it would be under statutes.

4. If further use of the provision or analysis is necessary, then obtain the cite to the Texas Code.

5. Read the provision and cite from the Texas Code itself and not from any information from Martindale-Hubbell.

Computer Note

LEXIS-NEXIS provides access to *Martindale-Hubbell* and other files for government, corporate law, specialties, and international attorney sources. **WESTLAW** maintains a Legal Directory profiling law firms, branch offices, and biographical records of lawyers in all fifty states, as well as government and corporate law offices. *Martindale-Hubbell* is on the **Internet** and may be accessed through <http://www.lawyers.com/site/home.asp>. There are a number of other companies such as West Legal Directory at <http://www.hg.org/attorney.html#west> and Legalserv at <http://www.hg.org/attorney.html#legalserv>.

APPENDIX

Sample Research Problems

Problem I

FACTS

Jane Smith sought a job as a marketing assistant for a large food processing company in Dallas, Texas. In accordance with company policy, Smith was required to complete successfully a drug screening examination conducted by an independent laboratory, Testco. Smith provided Testco with a urine sample and indicated on the medical history form that she was using no drugs. Nevertheless, her test results indicated the presence of opiates and, as a result, Smith did not get a job offer. After doing her own research, Smith learned that eating poppy seeds can cause a positive drug test result; Smith had eaten several poppy seed muffins in the days before the test. Testco did not advise Smith prior to the drug test that poppy seeds are a known cause of positive test results.

Jane Smith consults your law firm to determine whether there is a cause of action against Testco for negligence in failing to inform her prior to the drug test of the likely effect of ingesting poppy seeds on the test results.

RESEARCH ASSIGNMENT

Describe the nature of the authority you seek and the reason(s) you have selected that authority. Next, discuss the most efficient research tools which you will select to find, update, and verify the authority.

OUTLINE OF THE SUGGESTED RESEARCH PROCESS

The authority appropriate to this problem is primary mandatory authority in the form of Texas case law. This type of authority can be found in Texas appellate decisions through the steps described below:

1. Analyze the facts according to the TAPP rule.

2. Find the appropriate case law in the *Texas Digest, Second Series,* by using:

    a. Descriptive Word Method: Use key words and phrases, such as "negligence" and "drugs" in the Descriptive Word Index and pocket part to identify appropriate topic and key numbers; or,

    b. Topic Method: Go to the digest volume and pocket part covering the relevant issue, and examine the topic "Analysis," which is like a table of contents of the topic and key number subjects. Select the most appropriate key number(s).

3. Read the case summaries below the relevant key number(s) and get cites to cases closest in their facts to the client's problem.

4. Locate and read the case(s) in the appropriate *Southwestern Reporter* volume(s) and advance sheets.

5. Shepardize in *SHEPARD'S Texas Citations*, case volumes.

6. Consult the Subsequent History Table in:

  (a) the annual paperbound volume;

  (b) the advance sheets, *Southwestern Reporter*, Texas Cases; and,

  (c) the *Texas Supreme Court Journal* (weekly).

Problem II

FACTS

Your fourteen-year-old sister, currently living in Texas with your mother, just started high school and has decided to get a tongue stud in an effort to impress her new friends. Your mother is adamantly opposed and told your sister that she needs a parent's permission to get a tongue stud. Your sister wants you to determine whether she does, in fact, need parental consent.

RESEARCH ASSIGNMENT

Identify the nature of the authority you seek and the reason(s) you have selected that authority. Next, discuss the appropriate research tool(s) which are necessary to find, update, and verify the authority.

OUTLINE OF THE SUGGESTED RESEARCH PROCESS

The authority appropriate to this problem is primary mandatory authority in the form of a Texas statute. This authority is located in the annotated state statutes and can be located using the following steps:

1. Analyze the facts according to the TAPP rule.

2. Find the provision through any of the following methods:

    a. Popular Name Method: Use the popular name table in the Annotated Texas Statutes paperbound General Index if you have a popular name;

    b. Topic Method: Go to the individual subject index if you already know which code contains the provision; or,

    c. Descriptive Word Method: Go to the paperbound General Subject Index to look under "body piercing."

3. Read the provision in the Annotated Texas Statutes. Note the language regarding the effectiveness date of the legislation.

4. Update the statute by:

    a. the annual pocket part, unless the code is paperbound;

    b. pamphlet supplements (semi-annual);

    c. *Vernon's Texas Session Law Service* — Table 2, Statutes Amended or Repealed (regular paperbound issues in years that legislature convenes); and,

    d. *SHEPARD'S Texas Citations*, statutes volumes.

5. Find interpretive cases, if any, by:

    a. *Index of Decisions* following the text of the statute;

    b. the appropriate Note of Decision number(s) in bound volume or paper pamphlet.

6. Update the cases by:

   a. the annual pocket part, unless the code is paperbound;

   b. any pamphlet supplements (semi-annual);

   c. the advance sheets of the *Southwestern Reporter, Second Series*, Texas Cases, Statutes Construed Tables;

   d. *SHEPARD'S Texas Citations*, cases volumes; and,

   e. the Subsequent History Table in:

    (1) the annual paperbound volume

    (2) the advance sheets, *Southwestern Reporter, Second Series*, Texas Cases (weekly); and,

    (3) the *Texas Supreme Court Journal* (weekly).

Problem III

FACTS

Fred Steady worked for Unidelivery Service as a mechanic, a position that required him to drive commercial vehicles. Although Steady had high blood pressure, he was erroneously granted a certificate required of him by the Department of Transportation, even though the regulations expressly prohibit those with Steady's condition from driving commercial vehicles. When his employer discovered the error, Steady was fired.

Steady has heard of the Americans with Disabilities Act and believes his discharge was in violation of the statute and seeks advice from your law firm.

RESEARCH ASSIGNMENT

Describe thoroughly the authority you seek and the reasons you have selected that authority. Discuss the relevant research tools necessary to find, update, and verify the authority.

OUTLINE OF THE SUGGESTED RESEARCH PROCESS

The authority appropriate for this problem is primary mandatory authority in the form of federal legislation, its legislative history and interpretive case law, and any federal regulations pertinent to the legislation and interpretive case law of those regulations.

1. Analyze the facts according to the TAPP rule.

2. Find the federal statutory provision using any of the following methods:

    a. Popular Name Method: Use the popular name table in the paperbound *U.S.C.A.* or *U.S.C.S.* General Index to get the cite to the Americans with Disabilities Act;

    b. Topic Method: Go to the individual subject index if you already know the statute is in the Public Health and Welfare Code; or,

    c. Descriptive Word Method: Go to the paperbound General Subject Index with the words that you isolated during the TAPP analysis.

3. Read the federal statute in the bound volume or pamphlet of the *U.S.C.A.* or *U.S.C.S.* Note the public law number and any reference to a legislative history, such as a committee report published in the *U.S. Code Congressional and Administrative News* (*U.S.C.C.A.N.*). Be sure to verify the legislation's effectiveness date as well.

4. Check the legislative history sources available through:

    a. references to the *U.S.C.C.A.N.* edited materials, if any; or,

    b. Congressional Information Service (C.I.S.) annual legislative history volume for the year of the law's enactment referenced through the statute's public law number.

5. Update the statute:

    a. check the annual *U.S.C.A.* or *U.S.C.S.* pocket part, unless the code is paperbound;

    b. check pamphlet supplements;

    c. check the unofficial session laws, such as *U.S.C.C.A.N.*; and then,

    d. Shepardize the statute in *SHEPARD'S Federal Statutes Citations*, statutes volume.

6. Find interpretive cases:

    a. check the Notes of Decision in the bound volume, if any;

    b. check the Notes of Decision in the pocket part, if any;

    c. check the Notes of Decision in any supplementary pamphlet;

    d. check the Cumulative Table of Statutes Construed in advance sheets of all federal court reports; and,

    e. Shepardize any relevant cases in the appropriate *SHEPARD'S* volumes.

7. Locate interpretive rules or regulations, if any, in the *Code of Federal Regulations (C.F.R.)* by:

    a. The Parallel Table of Authorities in the annual *C.F.R. General Index and Finding Aids* volume using the U.S. Code title and section number located above to cross reference the applicable *C.F.R.* title and part number.

    b. Descriptive Word Method: Go to the annual paperbound *C.F.R. General Index and Finding Aids* volume with the words that you isolated during the TAPP analysis.

    c. Topic Method: Go to the appropriate title in the *C.F.R.* if you know which of the fifty titles is applicable.

    d. Agency Method: Because you know which agency enforces the rules, consult the list in the annual *C.F.R. General Index and Finding Aids* volume for the title and part numbers of the Department of Transportation.

8. Read the regulation(s) and note the cite to the enabling legislation.

9. Update the regulation(s) by:

    a. The supplementary pamphlet: Check the monthly *C.F.R. List of Sections Affected*; and,

    b.   The most recent daily *Federal Register* cumulative list of sections affected.

10.   Find interpretive cases by:

    a.   *SHEPARD'S C.F.R. Citations* for federal court decisions; or,

    b.   federal agency publications for any federal agency decisions.

11.   Update the judicial or agency decisions by:

    a.   *SHEPARD'S* citations for the relevant federal reporter; or,

    b.   *SHEPARD'S United States Administrative Citations* for federal agency decisions.

Problem IV

FACTS

Mr. Onsight lives in Bexar County, Texas. On December 31, 1984, his vehicle registration expired, so on that day he went to the Department of Motor Vehicles and renewed his registration. However, when he received his registration statement, which included the payment form, the clerk had itemized:

$22.00 registration fee

$5.00 optional registration fee

Mr. Onsight complained about this new optional fee because he thought it applied to persons who registered after January 1, 1985. The clerk told him that it could be imposed on December 31, 1984, because vehicle registrations could have been purchased the month prior to January 1, 1985, and therefore the assessment was proper.

In order to get his registration, Mr. Onsight paid the total amount, which included the $5.00 optional fee. However, he seeks your law firm's advice on this matter because he does not feel the state and Bexar County have authority to create such a statute or to collect this fee. Furthermore, he feels there is a conflict in the meaning of the word "month" in the statute in which the fee was imposed.

From newspaper accounts, your law firm knows that this fee was hotly debated even after extensive hearings, but that the legislation, whose popular name is the Vehicle Registration Act, was finally passed. Also, although the researcher is not familiar with the Department of Highways, he suspects that the county tax assessor is simply following instructions by the Texas Department of Highways and Public Transportation.

RESEARCH ASSIGNMENT

Describe thoroughly the nature of the authority you will seek and the reasons you have selected that authority. Be sure to discuss *all relevant* authority. Next, discuss the most efficient research tools which you will select to find, update, and verify all necessary authority.

OUTLINE OF THE SUGGESTED RESEARCH PROCESS

The researcher should begin the process by searching for primary mandatory authority. For example, Mr. Onsight questions whether the state has the authority to impose such a fee. Statutory authority is obtained from the Texas Constitution which gives the legislature power to act. Therefore, the Texas Constitution would have to be checked. In addition, because this is a legislative problem, the statute itself and any legislative history should be reviewed in the annotated code, *Vernon's Annotated Texas Statutes* (*VATS*). Furthermore, any rules and regulations implementing the statute should be located in the Texas Administrative Code.

Finally, relevant interpretive case law for the constitution, statute, and administrative regulations should be found, verified, and updated.

This problem also raises issues that make some secondary authority relevant. For example, Attorney General Opinions are valuable in this problem because the Attorney General is the legal advisor to the state and administrative agency. Although the opinion is not binding, it is very persuasive. To clarify the word "month," the researcher should use the secondary sources for resolving a definitional problem. These include a local encyclopedia, *Words and Phrases,* and a legal dictionary.

The Texas Constitution

1. Analyze the facts according to the TAPP Rule.

2. Use the key words and phrases in the Index to the constitutional volumes of *VATS*.

3. Read the provision in *VATS* constitutional volumes.

4. Review the relevant research aids and historical notes that follow the relevant section.

5. Update the constitutional provision by:

    a. the pocket part (annual);

    b. any pamphlet supplements (semi-annual); and,

    c. *SHEPARD'S Texas Citations,* statutes volumes.

6. Find appropriate case law, if any. This is accomplished by:

    a. looking at the *Index of Decisions*;

    b. finding a pertinent Note of Decision number in the bound volume; and,

    c. reading and analyzing the cases.

7. Update the cases by:

    a. the pocket part (annual);

    b. any pamphlet supplement (semi-annual);

    c. *SHEPARD'S Texas Citations,* case volumes; and,

    d. the Subsequent History Table in:

        (1) the paperbound volume (annual);

        (2) the advance sheets of the *Southwestern Reporter, Second Series,* Texas Cases (weekly although cases are three to six weeks old); and,

        (3) the *Texas Supreme Court Journal* (weekly).

Statutory Materials

1. Find the provision by:

    a. Popular Name Method: Although the popular name of the statute is given, there is no popular name table in *VATS*. However, the statute might possibly be found through *SHEPARD'S Acts and Cases by Popular Names*;

    b. Descriptive Word Method: Go to the General Subject Index and its supplements if you do not know where to look; or,

    c. Topic Method: Go to the Individual Subject Index and its supplements if you have some idea of the topic.

2. Read the provision in *VATS*.

    a. Note the language regarding the effective date of the legislation. Effective dates can be important in this problem because Mr. Onsight questions the date the fees were imposed.

    b. Because the problem states that there were debates and hearings, you should locate and review the legislative history:

      (1) use the Legislative Reference Library in Austin;

      (2) use a commercial service, *i.e.*, Legislative Intent Research; and,

      (3) note that Legislative Journals would NOT be helpful in this case because there are neither floor debates (they are taped) nor committee reports.

3. Update the statute by:

    a. the pocket part (annual);

    b. pamphlet supplements (semi-annual);

    c. *Vernon's Texas Session Law Service* (monthly); and,

    d. *SHEPARD'S Texas Citations,* statutes volumes.

4. Find interpretive case law by:

    a. the *Index of Decisions*;

    b. the appropriate Note of Decision number in the bound volumes.

5. Update the cases by:

    a. the pocket part (annual);

    b. any pamphlet supplements (semi-annual);

    c. the advance sheets of the *Southwestern Reporter, Second Series*, Texas Cases, Statutes Construed Table;

    d. *SHEPARD'S Texas Citations,* case volumes; and,

    e. the Subsequent History Table in:

      (1) the paperbound volume (annual);

      (2) the advance sheets, *Southwestern Reporter,* Texas Cases (weekly although cases are three to six weeks old); and,

      (3) the *Texas Supreme Court Journal* (weekly).

Administrative Materials

1. Check the *Texas State Directory* to obtain any information regarding the authority/function of the Department of Highways and Public Transportation or its director. This should be checked because the problem states that the researcher is not familiar with the Department.

2. Find the regulation in the *Texas Administrative Code* (*T.A.C.*) using one of the following methods:

   a. If you know the name of the agency, use the Table of Agencies. In this problem, the name of the agency (Texas Department of Highways and Public Transportation) is given and would be the quickest way to find the information.

   b. If you do not know the name of the agency, use the general subject/topic method. Consult the Table of Titles and Chapter Headings. It will direct you to the general subject matter contained in each title. From there, you can find the name of the agency. Then look at the General Subject Index at the back of the title which will give you more specific information.

3. Having found the appropriate title and chapter, consult the analysis which appears at the beginning of the title or chapter to find the heading number of the appropriate rule.

4. Read the relevant section in *T.A.C.*, if any.

5. Review the Source Notes which gives the history of each rule. Again, this is important to check in this problem because Mr. Onsight questions the effective date. See, e.g.:

   a. how the rule was adopted;

   b. when it became effective; and,

   c. where it was published in the *Texas Register*.

6. Citations of Authority provides the statutory or other authority by which an agency's rules have been issued. This is important in the current problem because Mr. Onsight questions the state and local authority to formulate such rules and fees.

7. Update the rule or regulation by:

   a. Certification Date Reference Table;

   b. *Texas Register Index — T.A.C. Titles Affected*, issued in print quarterly and monthly, and updated on the Secretary of State's website weekly; and,

   c. *Texas Register* individual issues, to read the changes — issued in print and on the Secretary of State's website twice weekly.

8. Find and update interpretive cases:

   a. Digest Volume: Use the basic descriptive word method in the *Texas Digest* to locate interpretive cases because the *T.A.C.* provides no Notes of Decision.

   b. Reporter Volume: Read the case in the appropriate reporter. If no cases are cited in the *T.A.C.*, the reader might go to the descriptive word index and employ the usual research process for interpretive cases.

   c. Shepardize any relevant cases in the appropriate *SHEPARD'S* volumes.

Secondary authority

1. Attorney General Opinions:

   a. find an opinion through the separate index pamphlet; and

   b. read the opinion in the bound volume.

   * Texas Attorney General opinions cannot be updated through *SHEPARD'S*.

2. To clarify the word "month," use the research sources for resolving a definitional problem. There are three possible sources to use:

   a. *Texas Jurisprudence* (1st, 2nd, 3rd);

   b. *Words and Phrases:*

   (1) state digests and pocket parts; or,

   (2) the series and pocket parts.

   c. *Black's Law Dictionary.*

Problem V

FACTS

Your client, National Medical Supply Company of Orlando, Florida, seeks your advice concerning the collection of $785,000 worth of medical supplies and equipment which it sold to John Bandit and Stanley Community Association of Medical Practitioners (SCAMP). On April 1, 1983, John Bandit contacted your client by mailing a newspaper ad and an order form to purchase medical supplies and equipment for SCAMP's new medical center. Two weeks later, Bandit mailed another order form for equipment and supplies to be sent to a second medical center. A third and final order was mailed one month later for equipment and supplies to be sent to a third facility. The three facilities that SCAMP ordered equipment for were located in three different states, but they were all within 100 miles of SCAMP's Florida headquarters. The purchases that SCAMP made for these three facilities totaled $785,000 in equipment and supplies.

The contract agreement called for payment to be made in three equal installments over a 90-day period. At the time of each installment, reminder notices were sent to Bandit and SCAMP by your client. However, none of the payments were made. Subsequently, six follow-up demand notices were sent to Bandit and SCAMP at monthly intervals. Neither Bandit nor SCAMP responded to the notices. Upon investigation, your client learned that SCAMP had defrauded the company by ordering medical equipment for nonexistent "front" hospitals which it then sold to other community medical clinics on fraudulent invoices.

The researcher knows that within the last two years the state legislature passed the Florida Racketeer Influenced and Corrupt Organization Act, or RICO, as it is commonly known. This provision is almost identical to the federal RICO statute which was designed to prevent a pattern of racketeering activity. Of special concern to both Congress and the Florida legislature was whether there would be constitutional problems if the statute was limited to "organized crime" or whether it should be extended to any "pattern" of racketeering. This issue was hotly debated in both committee proceedings and floor debates. The researcher is also concerned with the definition of "pattern of racketeering activity" and whether three "scams" would fall within that definition.

RESEARCH ASSIGNMENT

You have been asked to describe thoroughly the nature of the authority you will seek and the reasons you have selected that authority. Be sure to discuss *all relevant* authority. Next, discuss the most efficient research tools which you will select to find, update, and verify all necessary authority.

OUTLINE OF THE SUGGESTED RESEARCH PROCESS

The most important authority in this problem is primary mandatory authority. This type of authority can be found through the Florida Constitution, statutory provisions, and any Florida appellate court decisions that may interpret those provisions. Because the Florida RICO Act is relatively new and also because it is virtually identical to the federal RICO statute, legislative history or factually analogous cases at the federal level may be used if pertinent authority cannot be found in Florida. In addition, RICO violations may be brought under both the federal and state statutes, and consequently, constitutional, legislative, and judicial authority at both levels are relevant.

The use of selected secondary authority may be helpful. There are two limited reasons that secondary authority might be used. First, there is a question as to the definition of "pattern of racketeering" which needs to be resolved. Consequently, definitional resources such as a dictionary, the local encyclopedia, *Florida Jurisprudence,* or *Words and Phrases* may produce a case that defines whether as few as three scams are a "pattern" of racketeering. In addition, Attorney General Opinions at both the federal and state levels should be checked because the Attorney General is the legal adviser to the government and may have commented on this issue.

Secondary authority may also be useful in obtaining background information on the legislative history and intent of the federal and state legislatures. Although the regular means of finding legislative history should be explored, law review articles may provide insight into both the "organized crime" and "pattern of racketeering activity" issues. As a practical matter, there is a wealth of law review articles on RICO. It is somewhat unusual that so many journal articles have been written about a statute; this is primarily due to the heavy litigation that has taken place at the federal level.

Finally, as an additional source of cases or "practical pointers" for the practitioner, *A.L.R.* might be checked. The federal RICO statute was passed in 1970, and therefore, *A.L.R. Federal* would be the best starting point because it contains materials on federal issues since 1969. In addition, under the term "racketeer," the Index to Annotations has references to some annotations.

Constitutional issues

There are two constitutional questions that are raised in this problem: (1) whether the statutes are limited only to "organized crime," and are therefore unconstitutional; and, (2) whether the state has attempted to create "status crimes" which are also disfavored. Normally, the constitutional provision should be discussed first if there is a direct constitutional question. However, that is not the situation in this case. The easiest method of learning if a provision is constitutional is to check the Notes of Decision under the statutory provision. Consequently, this problem will be discussed at that juncture.

Florida legislative issues

1. Analyze the facts according to the TAPP rule.

2. Find the appropriate statute by:

   a. Popular Name Table Method: This method can be used because the researcher knows the name, RICO. Locate the statute by:

      (1) *West's Florida Statutes Annotated*;

      (2) *Table of Florida Acts by Popular Names* in *SHEP-ARD'S Florida Citations*, statutes volumes; or,

      (3) *SHEPARD'S Acts and Cases by Popular Names.*

   b. Topic Method: Use the Individual Subject Index (it will not be helpful in this problem); or,

   c. Descriptive Word Method: Use the key words and phrases in the General Index.

3. Normally, the researcher would read the relevant statutory provision in the bound volume. However, in 1981, the provision was renumbered as §§ 895.01 *et seq.*, and therefore, it does not exist in a bound volume. The text can be found in the pocket part of the bound volume.

4. Review the research aids that follow the relevant section. This provision was amended in 1984. Be sure to determine if the amendment affects your problem.

5. Update the statutory provision by:

   a. any pamphlet supplements;

   b. *West's Florida Session Law Service;* and,

   c. *SHEPARD'S Florida Citations*, statutes volumes.

6. Find interpretive case law by:

   a. Checking the Index to the Notes of Decision;

   b. Looking at the appropriate Note of Decision number in the pocket part because that is the first place the text is printed.

   c. Reading the relevant cases.

7. Update the case law by:

   a. *West's Florida Statutes Annotated,* pamphlet supplement;

   b. the advance sheets of the *Southern Reporter,* Florida Cases, Statutes Construed Table; and,

   c. *SHEPARD'S Florida Citations,* case volume.

Federal statutory issues

1. The same key words and phrases that were obtained from the TAPP rule can be used for the federal analysis.

2. Locate the relevant federal statute by:

   a. Popular Name Table in the *U.S.C.A.* which is located in the last volume of the General Index;

   b. *SHEPARD'S Acts and Cases by Popular Names*;

   c. Descriptive Word Method in the General Index; or

   d. Topic Method: Analyze the fifty titles of the U.S. Code. This will not be helpful unless the researcher knows that the civil provisions of RICO were in the criminal statutory provision, and that therefore, the relevant title is "Crimes and Offenses".

3. Carefully read the statute looking for particular language and any reference to legislative history.

4. Update the statute itself:

   a. check the pocket part;

   b. check the cumulative supplementary pamphlet (although none exists for the provision at issue in this problem);

   c. check the unofficial sessions laws; and,

   d. Shepardize the statute in *SHEPARD'S U.S. Citations,* statutes volume.

5. Find interpretive cases:

   a. check the Notes of Decisions in the bound volume;

   b. check the Notes of Decisions in the pocket part;

   c. check the Notes of Decisions in the cumulative supplementary pamphlet if available;

   d. check the cumulative Tables of Statutes Construed in the advance sheets of all federal court reports; and,

   e. Shepardize all relevant cases in the appropriate *SHEPARD'S* volumes.